GREG

RUB-LINE SECRETS

by Greg Miller

Edited by Patrick Durkin

© 1999 by
Greg Miller

All rights reserved. No portion of this publication may be reproduced or
transmitted in any form or by any means, electronic or mechanical,
including photocopy, recording, or any information storage and retrieval
system, without permission in writing from the publisher, except by a
reviewer who may quote brief passages in a critical article or review to
be printed in a magazine or newspaper, or electronically transmitted on
radio or television.

Published by

 **krause
publications**

700 E. State St. • Iola, WI 54990-0001
Telephone: 715/445-2214
fax: 715/445-4087
World Wide Web:
www.deeranddeerhunting.com

Krause Publications

Deer & Deer Hunting is a registered trademark of Krause Publications Inc.

Please call or write for our free catalog of outdoor publications.
Our toll-free number to place an order or obtain a free catalog is
800-258-0929. Please use our regular business telephone
715-445-2214 for editorial comment or further information.

Library of Congress Catalog Number: 99-61147
ISBN: 0-87341-812-3
Printed in the United States of America

Photography by Greg Miller and Jeff Miller
Pen-and-ink drawings by Chuck Miller
Hunting strategy drawings by Jennifer Pillath

Cover photo: Greg Miller with a Wisconsin bow-killed 9-point buck.

DEDICATION

In memory of Kevin Carriveau, a fellow hunter who left us too soon.

CONTENTS

ACKNOWLEDGMENTS

I thank God for the many blessings He has bestowed on me and my family. Thank you to my wife, Geralyn. Thanks for your encouragement, for your invaluable advice and assistance, and for always being there for me. I love you more than ever.

Thank you to my children, Jake and Jessie. I'm so glad you've had the opportunity to share in all this. Jake, you're the best son and finest hunting partner a father could possibly ask for. Jessie, you make me so proud. I look forward to the day you join Jake and me on our hunts.

Also, thank you so much to Gary Clancy, Gordon Whittington, Gerry Bethge, Bill Winke and especially Charlie Alsheimer. You guys all have helped me more than you could ever know.

And last, a special thank you to Patrick Durkin — both for your great editing skills and your loyal friendship. I'm convinced that knowing you has made me a better person.

ABOUT THE AUTHOR

Greg Miller was born and raised in whitetail-rich Wisconsin. Over the years his pursuit of trophy-sized bucks has led him to 14 other states and three Canadian provinces.

Almost the entire first 25 years of Miller's deer hunting life were spent chasing public-land whitetails in big-woods environments. But in recent seasons he has been striving to become more proficient at hunting big bucks from highly pressured farmlands.

If there's one thing quickly apparent about Miller's hunting style, it's his disdain for gimmicks and supposed shortcuts. He relies on dedication and hard work to consistently get within range of large-racked bucks.

Miller also believes in the common-sense approach to deer hunting. "Many deer hunters continue to fail because they're constantly out-thinking themselves," Miller said. "I've seen darn few deer hunting situations that couldn't be solved by applying a little common sense."

While he enjoys hunting whitetails in "exotic" locales, Miller spends most of his time near home hunting with his son, Jake.

In 1987, Greg Miller posed with these trophies, proof that he has been onto rub-line secrets for several years.

FOREWORD

Back in the days before I started working for *Deer & Deer Hunting* magazine, I could sit down with the magazine and just read it for fun and leisurely learning. There were no deadlines to sweat, no typographical errors to ruin an evening, and no printing snafus to stalk an unsuspecting staff.

Though it's now my job to worry about publishing's many gremlins, I've come to realize they don't matter if *D&DH's* readers don't eagerly await each issue's arrival in their mailbox. Whenever I need to remind myself that *D&DH* magazine is supposed to be educational *and* entertaining, I remember an article titled "Until Next Year" in the March 1990 issue of *D&DH*. That was my introduction to a great storyteller named Greg Miller. Don't get me wrong. I had read enough of Miller's earlier articles on deciphering rub lines and waylaying big-woods bucks to know his name and realize he was one serious hunting dude. But that's about all I knew of him. Until I read "Until Next Year," a story about Greg's unsuccessful sub-zero hunt for a monster whitetail, I had never seen the storyteller in him.

When Greg writes about his many insights into hunting big deer, he often claims anyone could have drawn the same conclusions. He also says anyone could match his consistent success on big bucks if they just worked hard. He even says he's simply sharing common-sense hunting tips. I appreciate his modesty, but all those claims are the storyteller side of him shining through. As I told Greg recently, to quote baseball great Paul Molitor, "If common sense were really that common, wouldn't everyone have it?"

Like it or not, most of us can learn a lot about deer behavior and hunting tactics from Greg Miller. We can trek through the woods and trudge through the swamps, recording every bit of deer sign we come across. We can even match him hour for hour on the tree stand, and again record every sight or sound the forest reveals. But when we go home and mull over what we've seen and heard, I doubt many of us would draw the same conclusions as Greg. As a result, our next move in the deer woods wouldn't be as decisive as Greg's.

That's why this book is so vital. If you put forth the required energy in the woods to know what sign deer are making, and when, where and how they're making it, Greg's insights in *Rub-Line Secrets* can provide the "why" part of the puzzle. From there, you can start to realize what Greg Miller would do if he were in your boots.

It's hard to argue with Greg's theories and beliefs about big-buck behavior. After all, the proof of his wisdom lies in his results. Over the years, he has consistently managed to read deer sign, devise a plan, and come home with impressive bucks. It can't all be coincidence, good luck or just hard work. Somewhere, the word *insight* figures heavily in the Greg Miller portrait.

After all, millions of deer hunters besides him were combing the woods in the 1960s and '70s. But how many besides Greg looked at rubs and saw vital clues to a buck's travel patterns? Remember, too, deer hunters of that era were reading articles and books by writer/hunters who considered rubs nothing more than random scars. Rather than accept that assumption, he analyzed the evidence and drew his own conclusions. Since then, he has consistently proven that rub lines can reveal a buck's travel routes between bedding and feeding areas. In effect, in about 15 years, Greg has taken us from thinking rubs are mere curiosities to believing they can often betray a buck's secret passages.

The key to his success is unique thought and analysis. When he finds two seemingly unrelated clues into big-buck behavior, he can quickly piece together the code that unlocks their meaning while others remain blind to the connection. And like other naturally talented people, he doesn't know why his observation-and-analysis skills don't come so easily to everyone.

In typical Greg Miller fashion, when he first considered doing a book on rub-line hunting, he wasn't sure he had enough material to fill the pages. Then, once he thought about the subject some more, he wasn't sure he could condense his thoughts into one book.

In *Greg Miller's Rub-Line Secrets*, Greg does everything except walk you into the woods and personally put you on a stand. If you read this book carefully, scout hard, hunt hard and apply his insights to your deer woods, you can't help but become a better rub-line hunter.

With that said, forget all you thought you knew about rubs and rub lines, and see them for the first time from Greg Miller's perspective. The woods and forests that harbor big bucks will never again look the same.

— Patrick Durkin
Editor, *Deer & Deer Hunting* magazine
August 1999

I made many mistakes in the late 1970s as I learned how to zero in on big bucks by interpreting their rubs and rub lines. Even so, I enjoyed some successful hunts as I developed my rub-hunting analysis, such as this 8-pointer I killed in 1980.

Chapter 1

WHY BUCKS RUB

M ore than 20 years have passed since I started using rubs and rub lines as aids in hunting white-tailed bucks. During my early rub-hunting attempts, I made more mistakes than any hunter should be forced to suffer.

Of course, when I first hunted rubs and rub lines during the late 1970s, I was on my own. There wasn't a bit of information available on the subject. In fact, I believe an article I wrote on rubs and rub lines in 1987 offered hunters the first practical information on the subject. That article proved deer hunters had a lot of interest in rubs and rub lines.

Before discussing how you can better use rubs and rub lines to hunt deer, it's important to discuss why white-tailed bucks rub in the first place. Even though deer hunters tend to be more rub-savvy than they were 10 to 15 years ago, many still misunderstand this aspect of buck behavior. Before you can increase your productivity — especially on mature bucks — it's important to acquire a basic, accurate understanding of why bucks rub. Once hunters gain that understanding, most realize it

Some rubs are visited and thrashed repeatedly by white-tailed bucks. A buck walking through his home area will often make a line of rubs that tips off his travel route.

would benefit them to increase their rub knowledge even more.

Rub Myths

To increase your rub knowledge, you must shed some myths. First, contrary to what you might think, bucks do revisit rubs; at least some of them. Second, bucks generally don't make deep, "serious" rubs while trying to remove antler velvet at summer's end. Rubbing associated with shedding velvet generally isn't intense. Bucks are simply trying to hasten the process and soothe an irritating source of itching. They really don't put their shoulders into it.

Rubbing is often done to help bucks unravel their hierarchal pecking order. A buck will often make a huge show of rubbing to demonstrate its strength and intimidate other bucks.

If you've heard or believed those two myths, you're not alone. Both supposed maxims were drilled into me nearly 30 years ago by a respected member of my father's deer hunting group. Although many years have passed since then, I still recall the old-timer's words: "Rubs don't mean a darned thing," he said. "They're just places where bucks tried to take the velvet off their horns. I don't think the bucks ever come back to those spots again." In defense of Dad's hunting partner, this was standard belief at the time.

Because of my faith in the old hunter, I assumed his thoughts on rubs were gospel. I believed his doctrine for at least the next decade. I then went through my enlightenment. Because of my ever-increasing interest in big bucks, I began spending enormous amounts of time in the woods during the off-season. Those intense scouting trips were instrumental in turning me into a successful trophy-buck hunter. My knowledge about several aspects of buck behavior greatly expanded, and No. 1 on my new-

---

Some bucks will use the same rubbing areas and established rub lines along the same routes each year because they've long provided safe passage.

---

knowledge list was rub behavior.

Some things I discovered were shocks to my system. For instance, I realized rubs were far more than places where bucks tried removing antler velvet. In fact, from what I could find, bucks didn't rub in earnest until after they had shed their velvet!

I also discovered bucks revisited certain rubs, sometimes frequently. What's more, I learned bucks sometimes lay out, figuratively speaking, rub lines across parts of their home range. Furthermore, some bucks used the same rubbing areas and established rub lines along the same routes each year.

This flood of rub-related information greatly benefited my hunting, but as I eventually learned, I had only begun to understand the rub-line connection.

The Intimidation Factor

Much of what I learn about rubs and rub lines comes by watching bucks make rubs. In fact, I've long believed one of the best ways to learn about whitetails is to simply sit and watch everything they do — and I mean everything! I zero in on every little thing bucks do before, during and after they rub. There's far more to rubbing than a buck lowering its head and doing mock battle with a bush, sapling or tree.

One aspect of rub behavior sticks out most to me and, interestingly, this behavior is seldom noted by most so-called deer experts. It's the intimidation factor. Whenever bucks get the chance, they rub to overtly intimidate other bucks. I liken this behavior to the flexing and strutting sometimes seen in weight rooms or teen-age boys approaching the water fountain. It's the "my muscles are bigger than yours" mentality.

Of course, bucks also use early-fall sparring matches to determine their place in the hierarchy. But I'm convinced the rubbing ritual plays a big role in establishing the bucks' pecking order. In fact, larger and more aggressive bucks can totally intimidate other group members purely through the sounds they make while rubbing. In fact, I've felt a bit intimidated at times by the sounds of a mature buck engaged in full-fledged rubbing. If you've never heard a mature buck rubbing, the sequence is

This was the smallest of three bucks that faced off in a field in Iowa that I could watch from my tree stand. This aggressive buck had a tremendously large neck and body, which seemed to intimidate its larger-racked adversaries. I took advantage of the buck's pugnacious attitude by rattling it into bow range.

I don't believe rubs act as no-trespassing signs or boundary markers in their home areas. While rubs provide visual clues to other deer, they hold the scent-markers of other bucks. When bucks rub, they leave behind odors from saliva, and forehead and preorbital glands.

A mature buck engaged in full-fledged rubbing can be intimidating. The sequence is filled with loud grunts and explosions of busting brush, breaking branches and grinding antlers.

filled with loud grunts and explosions of busting brush, breaking branches and grinding antlers.

These loud intimidation rituals fascinate me because most of the time mature bucks are shy and secretive. They seldom do anything to attract attention. Yet, by rubbing, they purposely make themselves obvious to anything and anyone within ear-shot. At first I couldn't figure out why a select few big bucks suddenly behaved so carelessly. But after studying the situations more closely, I realized those bucks were making their presence known for a reason. In every case I witnessed, another mature buck (or two) was somewhere nearby. I believe the larger buck was simply trying to intimidate its potential rivals with extensive and sometimes ridiculously loud rubbing sessions.

As you can probably guess, loud rubbing sessions almost always increase in frequency as the rut approaches. Then again, all rubbing activity increases as the rut approaches. Any buck with hard antler — from spikes to massive racks — increases its rubbing activity as autumn plays out.

The most obvious effect of all the rubbing is a dramatic increase in the bucks' neck sizes. With that increase comes a tremendous boost in strength of the bucks' neck muscles. I used to think the sole purpose for the increased size and strength was to help bucks hold their own in fights with each other — especially during the rut. The more I studied this subject the more I realized full-blown fights between mature bucks — or bucks of all ages, for that matter — were extremely rare.

So, if brawls between bucks are rare, why do they spend so much time pumping up? Again, I believe it's tied to intimidation factors. White-tailed bucks, especially mature bucks, usually do everything possible to avoid an actual fight. Much like weight-lifters, bucks strut their stuff to other bucks. They lay back their ears, fluff out their hair and walk stiff-legged while sidling alongside each other. After watching many of these encounters, I came to believe neck size is sometimes more of an intimidating factor than antler size.

White-tailed bucks, especially mature bucks, usually try everything possible to avoid a real fight. Much like weight-lifters, big bucks strut their stuff to make other bucks back down.

Little Big Intimidator

A bow-hunt in Iowa helps explain my belief. I was on a stand along the edge of a huge fallow field when a large-bodied deer appeared about 400 yards away. Bringing up my binoculars, I saw the deer had good-sized antlers. The rut had just kicked into gear, and mature bucks were in a frenzy, so I wasn't surprised when a second big buck walked into sight.

Minutes later, a third buck walked into the field. Because the bucks were far beyond bow range, I sat back to watch the fireworks. It didn't take long for the scene to blow up. The three males met at midfield and went into their muscle-buck routines. They flared their hair, pinned back their ears, and sidled stiff-legged past each other. One of the bucks was a solid 150-class 10-pointer, and another was close to 140. However, it was apparent the buck with the smallest antlers of the three was the most dominant. I could see his neck was swollen far more than the necks on the other bucks. I could also see that, although they were putting on a good show, neither of the other bucks wanted to take on the thick-necked buck.

Figuring I might be able to capitalize on its aggression, I made a loud rattling sequence. Less than a minute later the 130-class buck was standing 25 yards from my stand. The buck had a field-dressed weight of 250 pounds and its neck circumference measured 32 inches.

Over the years, I've had many opportunities to watch bucks steadily increase their neck sizes, starting from when they shed their antlers through the time they entered the rut. The transformation in their appearances sometimes bordered on unbelievable.

That reminds me of a big-woods deer I arrowed years ago. I first saw this buck on a late-August morning as I checked my bear baits. Although the buck was impressive in antler and body, its neck looked almost doe-like.

When I saw the buck a month later, its neck was only slightly larger. But when I arrowed the buck in early November, its neck had greatly swollen. When I measured its neck just behind the ears it encompassed a whopping 31 inches! And again, although several larger-racked bucks

All-out brawls are uncommon among white-tailed bucks. Most battles are merely a show of force in which bucks lay back their ears, raise their body hairs and sidle alongside each other in stiff-legged gaits. After sizing up each other, one usually backs down.

*Some intensely worked rubs are a
"communication center's" sign-post for bucks.
These rubs can be great places to wait for bucks.*

lived in the area, I had seen indications this buck was the boss

Rub Communication

It's now almost common knowledge that white-tailed bucks use rubs to communicate. However, contrary to what many hunters believe, rub communication isn't solely visual. Bucks leave a lot of scent on their rubs. As a buck approaches an already-rubbed tree, it first smells the rub. One sniff tells the buck which, if any, other bucks were there.

After it identifies the odors, the buck goes about scent-marking the rub. It usually starts by licking the rub tree, and then begins the actual rubbing process. While rubbing, the buck alternately rubs its forehead and antlers against the tree. Why? Bucks have a scent gland in their foreheads. When they want to thoroughly scent-mark a rub, they spend almost as much, or even more, time rubbing the tree with their forehead as with their antlers. This is why you'll often find hair imbedded in a rub tree's bark. Although uncommon, I've also seen bucks rub their preorbital (eye) glands on trees.

So, after identifying which bucks previously visited the rub, the buck leaves its own odorous calling card in the form of saliva, and scents from its forehead and preorbital glands. The next buck that visits will have no trouble identifying which buck(s) was there before.

"Boundary" Rubs

I've always doubted the theories that bucks make some rubs to mark their home territory. Supposedly, bucks make "boundary" rubs to visually warn other bucks that they're about to trespass on their turf. Some theories hold that you can identify the boundary rubs because they're the most intensely worked of all rubs, and because they appear on the largest trees.

I've walked through the core areas of hundreds of bucks during the past 20-plus years. Not once have I found evidence that a buck marked the boundaries of its home turf with rubs. Of course, I'm sure someone might say the boundary rubs were there and that I just didn't find them. No way! When I scout, I make sure I'm intimately familiar with my hunting areas. While following the rub lines of hundreds of different bucks, I've found nothing to suggest the rubs were mapping a boundary.

While I know bucks will make individual rubs to warn or intimidate "strange" bucks, we shouldn't overlook another common purpose for these rubs. That is, I believe some intensely worked rubs serve as a "communication center's" sign-post for resident bucks. Although some sign-post rubs are far from other deer- activity areas, they can be great places to wait for bucks.

For example, I once sat on a morning stand within bow range of a well-used sign-post rub on a 4-inch-thick pine. During a 30-minute period, five different bucks visited the rub. The first two bucks were 120-class 8-pointers. I considered them to be borderline "shooters" and

I believe rubs are far more helpful than scrapes for discovering where big bucks live and how to get close enough to kill them with a bow. I also believe rubs provide more critical clues about the comings and goings of mature bucks in my hunting area.

let them pass. The next three bucks were smaller. Regardless of their size, however, each buck performed the same ritual at the sign-post. They first smelled and licked the rub. Then they thoroughly rubbed their forehead and both antlers against the pine. Just before walking away, they smelled and licked the rub one more time.

I just wished the 16-point buck that lived in the area (I picked up its matched sheds the previous spring) would have visited the sign-post rub that morning. It never did show up.

Hunting Rub Lines vs. Scrapes

While all rubs aren't created equal, I believe that when you consider all the rubs you find in an area, you'll unlock some vital secrets. I remember an incident from the early 1980s when my brother Mike and I were scout-

Scrapes typically reveal little more than if bucks are present. Rubs, however, help determine the presence and size of bucks, and pinpoint a big buck's travel routes.

ing a section of forest in northern Wisconsin. I was showing a lot of interest and getting vocal each time we found a fresh rub. Finally, my brother could no longer take it.

"You pay a lot more attention to rubs now than you ever did before," he said. "You've caught onto something, haven't you?"

Mike, of course, knew I had been having good success on big bucks in recent bow seasons. He also knew my success was somehow a result of a new-found ability to read and decipher buck sign. What Mike didn't know was that contrary to what most hunters were doing at the time, I wasn't picking my stands on scrapes.

Although I was still in the infancy of my rub-line theories at the time, I knew enough to explain a few basic, common-sense beliefs. I also explained why I was rapidly losing interest in scrapes.

"For one thing, I'm not seeing as much big-buck activity near scrapes as I am around rubs," I said. "Also, I've found I can usually find out quickly if a big buck is hanging around an area by studying rub sign. I was never able to do that with scrapes."

I firmed up many of my initial beliefs about rubs during the next few years. Those findings proved that concentrating on rubs when scouting and hunting was far more beneficial than worrying about scrapes. Yes, achieving consistent success on mature bucks in the big woods means becoming a master at interpreting sign. However, you also must know which sign provides the most helpful, accurate information.

The only thing you can always decipher from scrapes is if there are bucks in the vicinity. Rubs, on the other hand, can help you determine the presence and size of bucks, and help pinpoint a big buck's travel routes. You can even use rubs to keep tabs on individual bucks. I'll cover that subject in depth later in the book.

That's not to say I totally ignore scrapes. I don't. While most of my big-buck scouting and hunting revolves around rubs, I prefer to hunt rub lines that also hold some scraping activity. Finding that combination on a travel route is usually a tip-off of higher-than-normal buck travel. Your chances for success are much higher whenever you set up in such places.

Greg's Practical Points

➤ *Contrary to popular opinion, white-tailed bucks will return to rubs. In fact, bucks revisit and use some rubs and rub lines every year.*

➤ *Bucks don't intensely rub when trying to hasten velvet shedding and relieve its associated itch. Rubs worth monitoring are made after bucks shed their velvet.*

➤ *Rubs aren't made to define the boundaries of a buck's home area. However, individual rubs can be the hubs for scent and visual communication between many bucks. These rubs are called sign-posts.*

➤ *Rubs are better than scrapes for determining if big bucks are in the area.*

➤ *Seek rub lines that include scraping activity along the route. This combination indicates above-average buck travel, and higher odds for hunting success.*

My son knows that no matter how much he learns from me about rubs and rub lines, he still must gather his own field observations to take advantage of my words. I can offer a "blueprint" of buck/rub behavior, but each hunter must build his own game plan to capitalize on the situation in his hunting area.

Chapter 2

BUCK/RUB
RELATIONSHIPS
THROUGH THE
SEASONS

While it's important to understand why bucks make rubs, it's equally important to at least basically understand how bucks relate to their rubs and rub lines the entire season.

While presenting deer hunting seminars the past 10 years, I've been asked hundreds of questions about all aspects of deer hunting. Besides wanting to know the hunting equipment I prefer, hunters seem especially interested in increasing their knowledge about rubs. They want to hear — in plain, easily understood language — how bucks relate to their rubs,

White-tailed bucks in velvet will relate to rubs and rub lines. Further, because these bucks are settled into a home range, they follow much the same early-season patterns in ensuing years, provided certain food and habitat factors remain constant.

whether it's Labor Day or New Year's eve.

I'll do my best to explain my thoughts and observations on the buck/rub relationship from late summer to winter, but here's the catch: The best I can do is create certain images and ideas in your mind, and provide a blueprint of a "normal" buck/rub relationship. You must realize there will always be bucks and situations that stray from the norm. After all, we're talking about mature whitetails here.

Therefore, you must complete the picture I start. To thoroughly under-

I join my brother Jeff in admiring an early-season prize, proving that sometimes it's worth putting up with insects and dense vegetation. It might be difficult to find an active rub line in the early bow season, but once located, these rub lines can provide the season's hottest action.

stand specific buck/rub relationships, you must complement your book-learned knowledge with a lot of in-the-field experiences and observations.

Field work is critical for two reasons. First, regardless of how carefully and thoroughly I try to explain an aspect of buck behavior, some important points seem to always get lost in translation. Second, remember you're dealing with a mature buck, an animal that has been influenced by years of experience, learned behavior and site-specific circumstances.

In other words, don't expect all big bucks to display an identical relationship with their rubs.

When the Connection Starts

The buck/rub relationship starts before bucks shed their velvet. You

One reason bucks tend to become especially reclusive and hard to hunt during early to mid-October is a sudden influx of bow-hunters, waterfowlers and small-game hunters. Deer see all this activity as human interference and take evasive action.

The pre-rut is a great time to set up along an active rub line near feeding areas, as this bruiser buck illustrates. New rubs and rub lines can appear almost daily. This is also a good time to scout new areas to quickly pinpoint the hottest buck travel corridors.

read that right. I believe white-tailed bucks start relating to rubs and rub lines before they shed their velvet. I assume some of you are raising an eyebrow in disagreement, and I understand your skepticism. Only recently did I become aware that bucks in velvet do indeed relate to rubs and rub lines. In fact, I get a bit embarrassed when I realize how long I was watching bucks in velvet relate to rubs and rub lines before I caught on to the obvious. After giving the matter much thought, I realized their behavior was normal. I also soon realized that — provided certain factors remain constant — I would see bucks duplicating the behavior in consecutive years.

Here's why. As everyone knows, white-tailed bucks are creatures of habit. Without much variability, they live in the same ranges, bed down in the same places, and frequent the same feeding areas year after year. As a result, velvet-antlered bucks often relate to rubs and travel along rub lines.

I no longer believe it's fruitless to hunt along rub lines when the rut is in high gear. I have found in recent years that big rutting bucks do, indeed, often follow rub lines.

Rub-line hunting can be futile during the October lull. Even so, waiting in ambush along active rub lines is likely the most productive tactic during this slow time.

They're simply using parts of their ranges and traveling corridors that have proven safe and secure. Rubs and rub lines in such places are not fresh, but were made in previous years. Let me assure you bucks will relate to rubs and rub lines from earlier years.

What's the value of such information? In past years I've bow-hunted three states and two Canadian provinces where bow season opened while bucks were still in velvet. It was important to know something about previous rub lines when hunting those places. It also proves priceless in my home state, Wisconsin, when I must do my early-season scouting weeks in advance.

Early-Season Rub Relationships

Bow-hunters, especially, need to realize that bucks relate heavily to their rubs and rub lines early in the season. To be blunt, however, few bow-hunters have learned how to effectively hunt early-season rub-lines. Granted, finding and figuring out an active rub line at this time of year can be tough.

Then again, all early-season bow-hunting can be tough. I can't think of another time during deer season when hunters must deal with so many variables. Besides sometimes ridiculously hot temperatures, bow-hunters also must contend with dense, leaf-covered underbrush and hordes of insects, biting and otherwise. Even so, I still consider the early season one of the best times to ambush a big buck along a rub-line.

The trick to early-season effectiveness is to learn how to use the positive factors to your benefit. For instance, in most parts of whitetail country, white-tailed bucks are still in bachelor groups and living inside their core areas when bow season opens. What's more, these bachelor groups will be in predictable feeding patterns. By predictable, I mean most buck movements will occur between their bedding areas and preferred feeding areas. Their preferred bedding/feeding routes can be identified by active rub lines. Hunting along active rub lines at this time could put you in position to see nearly every buck in a given area!

If you don't get out into the woods during the late bow season, you'll never know how productive rub lines can be in the post-rut. Unfortunately, many hunters write off the late season, not realizing that bucks often return to their pre-rut trails.

Rub Relationships for October's Lull

Hunters who think the early season is the most difficult time to arrow a mature buck haven't hunted much during the dreaded October lull. With the possible exception of some parts of the post-rut period, there's no other time mature buck movement is so suppressed. Even rub-line hunting can be futile during the October lull. Given the circumstances, however, waiting in ambush along active rub lines is likely the most productive tactic available during this slow time.

Allow me to explain. I believe several factors cause bucks to become extra secretive and daylight-shy during the lull. One reason is the sudden influx of hunters into deer habitat. This often-intense pressure isn't just from deer hunters. Small-game and waterfowl hunters also figure in.

As intense as this extra pressure might be, however, it's not the only reason big bucks suddenly go underground. In fact, even where hunting pressure is light, big bucks remain reclusive during the October lull. I believe this annual behavior pattern could be called the lull before the storm. I think bucks are resting in order to be in the best possible physical condition for the rut.

Bucks at this time severely restrict their travels while greatly increasing their intake of nutritious foods. Unfortunately for hunters, bucks spend little time traveling and feeding in daylight during the October lull.

In addition, mature bucks are never more attuned to their surroundings

Most buck travel during the pre-rut occurs along active rub lines. But unlike in early autumn, big bucks are now significantly more active in daylight.

than they are during the lull. They miss little that occurs in their core areas, including the comings and goings of less-than-careful bow-hunters. Still, even with lowered expectations, it's possible to enjoy some success during the lull. You must recognize when bucks go into the lull, and then act accordingly.

Setting up along active rub lines can be the hottest act in a lukewarm play. Just remember that the sparse daytime buck activity that does occur will typically take place within bow range of bedding areas. That applies to morning and evening activity.

Pre-Rut Rub Relationships

The pre-rut is the best time for rub line hunting. At no other time do bucks relate so strongly to their rubs. By "pre-rut," I'm referring to those 10 days immediately before the first does start entering estrus. During this time, bucks also relate to staging areas and sign-post rubs, but they relate big time to rub lines. What I find most exciting about this time period is that fresh rubs continue to appear almost daily. This steady supply of fresh sign can help you pinpoint the exact location of the area's most preferred big-buck travel routes. I've also used these rub explosions to quickly figure out new hunting areas. Even if I have only a little time to hunt, I'll often avoid a new area until the final week of the pre-rut. With bucks regularly laying down the most fresh sign of the year, I'm confident it won't take long for me to locate several productive stand sites.

As with the early season and the October lull, the bulk of buck travel during the pre-rut occurs along active rub lines. But unlike those earlier periods, big bucks are now significantly more active in daylight. Granted, during the first stages of the pre-rut, you still might need to place your rub-line stands close to buck bedding areas. But relax this "rule" gradually as the pre-rut progresses. During the pre-rut's final days, I often place my stands near the edges of feeding areas. Monster bucks spend a lot of time prowling in daylight near feeding areas just before the rut.

If you've read any of my early writings on rubs and rub lines, you

Post-rut bucks relate to their rubs and rub lines in much the same way they did during the early pre-rut. Although that fact is well-known today such information was priceless just a few years ago.

know I've long believed that rub-line hunting quickly becomes unproductive once the rut kicks into gear. I once thought bucks quit using their rub lines after the first does entered estrus, and that they didn't resume traveling along rub lines until after the last does were bred. But like a handful of my other beliefs on buck behavior, that observation hasn't stood the test of time. In recent years, my scouting and hunting suggests rutting bucks do, indeed, relate to rubs and rub lines.

Rub Relationships in the Post-Rut

For many years I believed the post-rut period was my least favorite time to hunt mature bucks. I've changed that thinking dramatically the past 15 years, possibly because my knowledge of rubs and rub lines increased greatly during that time.

As I eventually discovered, post-rut bucks relate to their rubs and rub lines in much the same way they did during the early pre-rut. Although that fact is mostly general knowledge today, I can't possibly begin to tell you how priceless such information was just a few years ago.

For the most part, Wisconsin's gun season and late archery season run during the post-rut. Before taking the time to increase my knowledge of rubs and rub lines, my success rate on big bucks was terrible during the gun season. I suffered the same dismal fate in the late archery season. Of course, that might be because I seldom, if ever, ventured into the woods during the late bow season.

My outlook changed dramatically once I learned how post-rut bucks relate to their rubs and rub lines. However, realizing success in the post-rut often entails doing more than just setting up anywhere along active rub lines. While it's possible some of your pre-rut stands along rub lines will be productive in the post-rut, an equal number will be duds. It will then be necessary to make slight adjustments to your rub-line hunting tactics. This is especially true when certain factors cause bucks to slightly alter their interactions with their rubs and rub lines.

We'll explore some of those situations later in the book.

Greg's Practical Points

➤ *Regardless of how carefully and thoroughly we discuss buck behavior, don't expect all big bucks to display an identical relationship with their rubs. Each mature buck has been influenced by years of experience, learned behavior and site-specific circumstances.*

➤ *Velvet-antlered bucks often relate to rubs and travel along rub lines. In many cases, these rubs will have been made in previous years. Bucks use travel corridors they've come to trust for safety and security.*

➤ *Early bow season can be a good time to kill a buck off a rub line because their movements are still fairly predictable. These bucks might also still be in bachelor groups and feeding in predictable patterns.*

➤ *The pre-rut is the best time for rub-line hunting. At no other time do bucks relate so strongly to their rubs. This time period occurs about 10 days before the first does enter estrus. Fresh rubs appear almost daily.*

➤ *Post-rut bucks relate to their rubs and rub lines in much the same way they did during the early pre-rut. However, while it's possible some pre-rut stands on rub lines will be productive in the post-rut, an equal number will be duds. Don't be stubborn. Move or adjust your stands accordingly.*

Hunters 30 years ago sometimes achieved excellent results during deer season because they took their exhausting work ethic into the woods. They typically considered rubs to be little more than curiosities. Not until the 1980s did some hunters begin to realize they could use rubs to figure out a buck's travel patterns. By the way, I actually appear in this photo. I'm the youngster (with a back tag) standing sideways in front of the hunter with the camera bag over his shoulder.

Chapter 3

READING INDIVIDUAL RUBS

As we discussed in Chapter 1, deer hunters 30 years ago commonly thought rubs meant nothing for determining practical, tactical hunting strategies.

Maybe you find it difficult to believe our hunting fathers could have been so unaware of rubs' significance. Before getting too judgmental, let's remember that even as little as 20 years ago, deer hunting was more commonly a once-a-year social event than it is today. In my home state, Wisconsin, for example, I would guess that nearly 90 percent of deer hunters a generation ago chased whitetails only during the annual nine-day firearms season. Only as bow-hunting mushroomed in popularity since the mid-1970s did we see widespread numbers of "year-round" hunters, not only in Wisconsin, but across the whitetail's range.

I will also point out that, despite their neglect of rub interpretations, my dad and his hunting partners did well each gun season. Although they

If hunters study rubs carefully and notice the differences between individual rubs, they can begin to figure out which buck is making which rubs. Bucks have different rub-tree preferences, and they will create distinct rubs that vary between bucks based on the size and configuration of their racks.

By learning how to read the "fingerprints" made by bucks when making rubs, I'm able to keep track of the movements of individual bucks. No matter where you hunt bucks, the ability to read rubs will help you pinpoint the travel patterns of different bucks in your area.

believed otherwise, they didn't know that much about their quarry. They did no scouting, took no precautions against human odor, made repeated trips into the same areas, and used what we would consider inferior weapons with open sights.

From our modern-day deer hunting perspective, we arrogantly think they did everything wrong. Still, for sheer numbers of deer shot and the trophy quality of their bucks, they succeeded where many of us still fail.

How did my father and his partners succeed so consistently? They applied their generation's exhausting work ethic to their hunting. They had an unwritten rule that unless you had shot a deer, you left camp before daylight and didn't return until after dark. Anything less than dogged determination marked a person as a casual deer hunter. A sandwich and soft-drink in their game-pocket was all they took to hold them over until the evening meal.

Contrary to that dogged approach, too many of today's deer hunters believe they'll do just as well by devouring vast reservoirs of information

Individual bucks often prefer different species of trees or brush for rubbing. I found this big rub on a healthy-size balsam fir in northern Wisconsin.

from the convenience of their easy-chair. They don't bust their hump, so to speak, in the woods and forests. If you're more of a reader/viewer than a scouter and walker, I have news for you: Consistent success on big bucks requires that you spend as much time in the woods as you do watching TV or reading books and magazines. As I always say, becoming book-smart about big whitetails will help, but only to a point. You still must know how to apply every scrap of your book-learned knowledge. The only way you can become a proficient hunter is by developing an intimidating work ethic!

In the previous chapter, I talked about how my successes on mature bucks improved once I paid more attention to rubs and less attention to scrapes. I didn't mention, however, that it took several years of intense study and hard work to grasp the basics of how bucks relate to their rubs and rub lines. My education was based mainly on the frustrations of trial and error. Fortunately, I tackled only one aspect of rub behavior at a time.

Rubs Help ID Bucks

Although every aspect of rub behavior intrigues me, I find one more interesting than all others. Maybe that's because it's one of the most helpful when pursuing big-woods whitetails. By studying rubs, I learned to use them to identify individual bucks. I've heard some hunters say that is worthless information. As a Midwestern bow-hunter once told me after a seminar: "You go into great detail on how to use rubs to identify bucks. How will that help me kill big deer?"

This guy must not have listened closely to that part of my seminar. I've chased big-woods whitetails since Day 1 of my deer hunting existence. Big-

The height of each rub above the ground is one clue that helps pinpoint which buck is making which rub. High rubs don't necessarily mean a long-legged buck, just as low rubs don't mean a stubby buck. Some bucks just like to rub higher on the tree than others. My brother Jeff found this rub on an aspen, or poplar, tree.

I suspected a buck in my hunting area was a nontypical because of scratches and gouges that appeared in odd places on rub trees. Not until the late bow season did I confirm my suspicions when I shot this buck. It had a basic 10-point rack with eight abnormal points.

Some bucks are more aggressive than others. They rub on larger trees, and they rub more savagely than bucks with passive temperaments.

---

woods bucks are far more reclusive and man-shy than their farmland cousins. This is especially true of mature bucks. Granted, the vastness of the big woods and forests makes it easier for big bucks to elude hunters. These factors also make it tougher to learn how bucks are using their range, or if certain areas even hold big bucks. However, I've learned to use rubs to help learn both of those things and to keep track of individual buck movements. Best of all, my ability to read rubs serves me well in every conceivable type of whitetail habitat.

Although it might not be quickly apparent, all bucks display somewhat different rubbing styles. For instance, some bucks are naturally more aggressive than others. They almost always make their rubs on larger trees, and they rub more savagely than bucks with more passive temperaments. Aggressive bucks are usually more "rub-active" than passive bucks. It follows, then, that rub lines made by these deer are relatively easy to find and follow. Unfortunately, these rubbing machines are not common. In fact, differences in rubbing styles from one buck to the next are usually subtle. That's why you must train yourself to notice the many subtle differences before you'll readily identify one buck's rubbing style.

What You Should Study

One easily understood identifier is the rubbing preferences bucks have for tree and shrub species. In fact, I think some bucks go out of their way to rub on a certain tree species. A monster big-woods buck I hunted for two seasons displayed such a trait. The massive 10-pointer had a penchant for rubbing 4- to 6-inch diameter spruce trees. I noticed his preference for spruce while following one of his rub lines when spring-scouting. Because of his somewhat passive temperament, I initially had a tough time unraveling his line of travel. That job became easier once I realized he was rubbing exclusively on spruce. Whenever I lost track of his rub line, I stepped back and studied the woods ahead. The predominant trees in this area were poplar and birch, so spruce trees stood out from the crowd. When I spotted a spruce, I tried to determine if it was the proper diameter. If it matched the buck's profile, I walked over and checked it. This relatively simple approach helped me unravel a rub line that was nearly a mile long. My efforts

Bucks that have long tines on their racks often make easily noticed scratches and gouges above, below and beyond the rubbed area of a tree or sapling. It's not unusual to find beaten up brush and saplings behind the main rub tree. If this damage occurs well behind the main rub tree, the buck likely has extremely long tines and will leave a recognizable pattern everywhere it rubs.

Some bucks in my region rub mostly on spruce, but others prefer poplars, balsam fir or white cedars. An occasional buck prefers red dogwood.

---

provided a reward: At the end of that rub line, near the edge of a major bedding area, I found both of his shed antlers.

That experience was one of the first in which I kept tabs on a big buck simply through his rubbing preferences. Since then, I've hunted countless other big bucks that displayed that trait. Some of those bucks also rubbed almost exclusively on spruce, but others preferred poplars, balsam fir or white cedars, while an occasional buck preferred to shove its antlers into clumps of red dogwood brush and destroy them. And though it's rare in my region, I've seen a couple of instances where big bucks went out of their way to rub certain fence posts.

Rub Fingerprints

It's also possible to keep track of individual bucks by the type of rub pattern, or "fingerprint," they leave on rub trees. For instance, one big buck my brother Jeff and I hunted for several seasons rubbed a distinct half-moon pattern into trees.

Without a doubt, the most memorable and easily identifiable rub pattern I've seen was made by a big-woods buck we hunted for several seasons. This buck almost always picked on huge spruce trees, and his fingerprint was gouges made very low on the tree. As luck would have it, a gun-hunter eventually shot this buck. A glance at his rack explained his rubbing tendencies. The main beams on the 160-class 11-point rack curved around and nearly touched in front. There's no way that buck could squeeze even a sapling between his main-beam tips. Instead of rubbing in the conventional manner, this buck improvised by using his long, bladed brow tines to gouge spruce trees. To do that, however, he tilted his rack so far forward that his nose must have nearly touched the ground. No wonder his rubs were so low! In case you're skeptical about that conclusion, we didn't find any more low rubs after this buck was killed.

More Rub Clues

Several years ago, my brother Jeff found an active rub line that is among the most unique I've ever seen. Jeff had found what he thought was the midpoint of the rub line, and recruited me to help locate its beginning and

---

Do I have a theory to explain why some bucks
rub high on trees? Yup. At risk of sounding flip,
some bucks just prefer to rub that way!

---

end. Jeff said the rub line was atop a steep wooded bluff in farm country near our homes. I knew the bluff held mostly mature red oaks and tall, straight poplars.

"But there are a few pine trees on top of the bluff, and that's what the buck is rubbing," Jeff said. It sounded as though the scouting job was going to be easy, and it was. The buck was indeed seeking and rubbing pine trees exclusively. But that only partly explains why scouting his rub line was so easy. For some reason, this buck consistently rubbed the pines a full 3 feet above the ground! In all my years of intense hunting and scouting, I have never seen a case where a big buck consistently rubbed so high. Talk about being able to identify a deer positively through his rubs! Do I have a theory to explain why the buck rubbed so high? Yup. At risk of sounding flip, that buck just preferred to rub that way. Nothing more.

Rubs Relay Antler Traits

Several years ago, I arrowed a massive 18-point nontypical during Wisconsin's late archery season. Though neither Jeff nor I ever saw this buck until the afternoon I shot him, we kept a fairly accurate record of his comings and goings for two years. We did this merely by monitoring his rub activity. This nontypical made easily identifiable rubs. Not only did he rub almost exclusively on·large poplars, but he always left fingerprint scratches and gouges on his chosen trees. Because the scratches and gouges were in weird places on the rub-trees, Jeff and I long suspected the buck had a rack that was at least slightly nontypical. As we finally discovered on a cold December afternoon, the buck was more than just slightly nontypical. His basic 10-point rack sported eight abnormal points, including a 6½-inch can-opener point that grew from the base of his left antler. No doubt, this abnormal point caused most of the weird scratches and gouges we had noticed on the rubs he made.

I believe certain antler characteristics will more quickly identify an individual's rub than any other factor. For instance, bucks with long tines often leave noticeable scratches and gouges well above and below the main rub. I've also seen many cases where long-tined bucks rubbed on one tree while inflicting coincidental damage on a tree or brush behind the main rub-tree.

No doubt, the rubs from long-tined deer are easy to identify.

Many of you have likely seen rubs where bark was frazzled and frayed. These are works of art, as far as I'm concerned, and make for the prettiest of rubs. They're also some of the easiest for fingerprinting bucks. These rubs are made by bucks with extremely heavy beading around their antler bases. Kevin Shibilski, a good friend and hunting partner, once kept track of a big buck for three years purely through the buck's extremely frayed rubs. Shibilski told me: "I nicknamed the buck 'Raspy' the first year because the trees he rubbed looked like they were worked over with a wood rasp. You could identify his rubs from a distance. They were just so different in appearance than all other rubs in my hunting area."

Some bucks make extremely raspy rubs, which indicates their racks are extensively pearled around the bases. I think raspy rubs are the prettiest rubs in the deer woods.

Rub Size/Buck Size Correlations

Because I'm often asked this question, I would be remiss if I didn't include my thoughts about correlating a buck's size to his rubs. Besides, I like talking about this topic. My theories for deciphering the big rub/big buck connection are based mostly on common sense, but I've corroborated my theories with solid in-the-field observations.

How does common sense factor into this question? Well, study a tine-gouged, bark-frayed rub on a 3-inch or larger tree. Do you think a spike-horn, forkhorn or even a basket-racked yearling can wreak extensive damage? If you're not sure, factor in the strength, aggressive natures and overall temperaments of young vs. mature white-tailed bucks. Common sense should be yelling, "No way!" Even healthy 2½-year-old bucks seldom take on large trees for long when they rub, at least not consistently.

That is the biggest reason I use rubs instead of scrapes as my main scout-

Tracks aren't good indicators of a buck's size. I believe rubs are much better indicators of a buck's size. Even a healthy 2½-year-old buck seldom takes on huge trees when it rubs. I consider any rub tree thicker than my wrist to be worthy of further study.

ing and hunting aid. Without question, large rubs are the most reliable way to determine if there's a big buck or two hanging out in an area. Some hunters will argue that they can use scrapes for the same purpose. They usually say: "I just look at the size of the tracks in scrapes. Big tracks always mean big bucks."

No they don't! I've seen big bucks with tiny hoofs, small bucks and does with huge hoofs, and deer with every hoof size in between. Tracks are a poor indicator of a deer's size, and they're not worth the dirt they're printed on for judging antler size. Rubs, on the other hand, have proven dozens of times to be accurate predictors of a buck's size and its antlers.

How big is big, where rubs are concerned? I consider anything wrist-sized and larger to be a big rub, or at least big enough to make me think the buck that made the rub is worthy of my attention. I didn't set the "wrist-sized" guideline on a whim. I studied, scouted and hunted rubs and rub lines intensely for years before adopting that guideline. I can think of only a handful of cases where I've been disappointed upon seeing the buck responsible for the wrist-sized rub I've hunted.

The Importance of Rub Identification

So why is it so important you learn to identify individual bucks through their rubs? I think I've already answered that question with my descriptions above. In case you missed it, though, consider this: If you can't distinguish one buck's rubs from another's, all you have is a confused collection of rub sightings. It's the individual traits of each rub that, when combined and analyzed, separate one buck's routine from another's.

In most cases, rubs are all you can go on until you see and kill the buck. Why? Once bucks reach a certain age, they become reclusive, man-shy and difficult to spot. You must rely on your sign-interpretation skills to keep track of them. When I hunt, I want to know exactly where these big bucks feed, bed and walk. Learning how to identify individual bucks through their rubs provides a reliable system to accomplish these tasks.

Greg's Practical Points

➤ *Consistent success on big bucks requires that you spend as much time in the woods as you do watching TV or reading books and magazines. The only way you can become a proficient hunter is to take an intimidating work ethic into the woods.*

➤ *Learn to identify individual bucks by their "fingerprint" on their rubs. If you can't distinguish different bucks by their rubs, all you have is a chaotic collection of rub sightings.*

➤ *One easy identifier of individual bucks is the rubbing preference each buck has for certain trees and shrub species. Some bucks go out of their way to rub on a certain tree species.*

➤ *Certain antler characteristics will more quickly identify an individual's rub than any other factor. For instance, bucks with long tines often leave noticeable scratches and gouges well above and below the main rub.*

➤ *Tracks are a poor indicator of a deer's size, and they're not worth the dirt they're printed on for judging antler size. Rubs, on the other hand, are accurate predictors of a buck's body size and its antlers.*

➤ *Rubs on trees wrist-sized and larger should be considered big, which means the rub's maker is worthy of your attention.*

Predicting where bucks will show up requires more than locating a few rubs and studying topographical maps. Hunters must understand how terrain, cover and the "edge effect" work together to concentrate deer movements and rub activity. Some of the busiest rub sites will be where ridgelines and points with "soft" covers converge. Soft edges are subtle changes in forest or cover type within the woods or forest. Areas where mature forests meet younger growth will usually produce the strongest edge effect.

Chapter 4

WHERE'S THE RUB?
A GUIDE TO LOCATING BUCKS

Author's Note: *I'm stepping aside momentarily to let you read some good hands-on rub research by Tennessee's Bryan Kinkel. Bryan shared his findings in the October 1997 issue of* Deer & Deer Hunting. *Because so many of Bryan's insights mesh with my own observations, I asked him to use this chapter to discuss his work.*
— Greg Miller

by Bryan Kinkel

Getting a good handle on buck movements is seldom as simple as finding a few rubs and then mapping the bucks' travel routines.

Most discussions of rub lines and travel patterns generally revolve

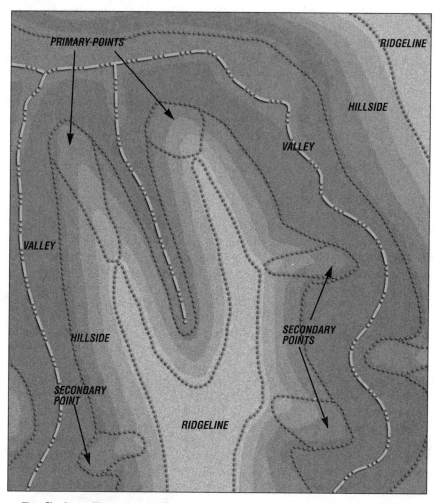

Defining Topography

We divided the topography into four primary classes: points, valleys, hillsides and ridgelines. Although not all terrain features could be classified into these categories, the categories covered most topography in the study area because few flat areas exist there. In reviewing the area's level areas, we grouped bottomlands with valleys, and level upland sections with ridgelines.

To be classified as a point, a bend in the topography had to create a corner of 90 degrees or less. We subdivided points further into primary points, defined as the end of ridges; and secondary points, defined as small points that descend from sides of ridges. To picture the difference between the point subdivisions, imagine a buck's antlers as a series of long, narrow ridges. The tips of the antler tines would be the primary points, while any stickers or nontypical points on the tines would be secondary points.

— Bryan Kinkel

around   two
common land-use
practices: farming
and forestry. In
agricultural areas,
rub lines can be
found along the
edges created by
fields,   funnels,
brushy draws and
fencerows. In big-
woods   environ-
ments,   rub-line
hunters often look
for creeks, streams,
swamps and other
drainage systems as
guides to buck
movement.

Influence of Edges on Rub Distribution

Legend: 0 to 10 meters / 10 to 20 meters / More than 20 meters

Y-axis: Rubs Per Acre (0–10); X-axis: Distance from Edge

Using a survey designed by deer researcher Grant Woods, Bryan Kinkel found that rub distributions were greatly affected by various types of edge cover. That influence, however, only extended about 10 meters. Rub densities were basically the same in areas 10 meters past an edge boundary.

A Case Study

After years of fruitlessly searching for rub lines that matched the edge patterns we often read about, my hunting partners and I became convinced that buck movement hinged on factors other than obvious edge locations. We found rubs along clearcuts and powerline right-of-ways, but these "hard" edges were few and far between on our land. Our property is characterized more by long sections of timber broken only by an occasional agricultural bottom-land.

We expected rub lines on our property to resemble big-woods patterns. But instead we found few rubs along drainage systems. Therefore, we concluded other factors were determining buck movement.

The distinguishing feature of our land is its rugged topography. Its rolling hills are characterized by a maze of long, narrow, meandering ridges, some of which run for miles. How could we more accurately use topography to help understand and predict buck travel routes?

You'll hear, for example, that bucks often move along valleys and up hillsides, following paths that take them gradually up the incline, almost parallel with the topography. Others suggest bucks often cross steep ridgelines at low points, such as saddles.

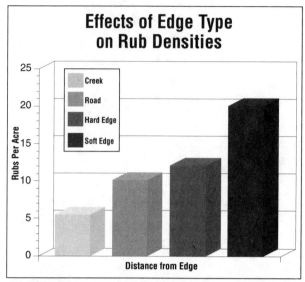

Effects of Edge Type on Rub Densities

Kinkel's rub survey revealed that edge types producing the strongest effect on rub distribution and densities were not the classic "hard" edges, such as field edges or powerline right-of-ways. The best producers were "soft" edges, such as the subtle changes in forest or cover type, especially where mature forests met younger growth.

Unfortunately, after several years of post-season scouting and mapping rubs, we found relatively few rub lines in valleys and even fewer on hillsides. We did find rubs in ridge-line saddles, but we also found concentrations of rubs along entire ridge-lines, not just the low spots.

Over time, these ridgeline rubs became the focus of our efforts to discover how topography influences buck movement. When we plotted and counted the rubs we found each year, we saw that most were made along ridgetops, which contradicted the theories we had been following.

A Rub-Density Survey

In 1994, our group placed the property under a quality deer management program. Since then, with the help and guidance of wildlife biologist Grant Woods, our management strategies produced older bucks and a better doe-to-buck ratio.

Woods also helped us compile a rub-density survey to test his theories about rub activity and frequency in herds with mature buck populations. His survey was designed to determine the average number of rubs per acre, and provide data on topography, average rub size, preferred rub-tree species, and the effects of edge and land use on rub distribution.

Our property was too large to canvass completely, but Woods' survey allowed us to collect an accurate sample of the area by placing random transit lines across the land. We checked for rubs on every bush, tree and sapling within 10 meters of both sides of each line, allowing us to take long, thin sample surveys of each terrain feature.

Before establishing the transit lines, we mapped the area into topographic and land-use categories. After laying and measuring the transit lines, we compared the percentage of deer travel with each topographic and land-use category. That ensured we had proportional representation of deer movements. We also divided edges into categories because we wanted to study the influence of the edge types on rub distribution.

Next, we assigned a category to each edge that was crossed by a transit line. We also checked the total and type of edges that intersected the property.

After the 1995 breeding season, I spent several weekends conducting the rub survey with my hunting partner, Jeff Roberts, and my father, Donald Kinkel. We walked the transits, measuring and recording every rub within 10 meters of both sides of the survey lines. We also recorded the land-use and topographic classifications of each rub's location. To measure the effect edges have on rub distribution, we measured and recorded the distance between each rub and the nearest edge, along with the edge's classification.

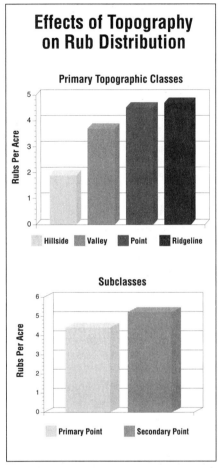

Because the landscape was similar across the study area, it might have altered some of Kinkel's findings. What can't be denied is the influence topography had on rub distributions. Rub densities for the different topographical features were, in rubs per acre: ridgelines, 4.7; points, 4.5; valleys, 3.7; and hillsides, 1.9. For the land-point subclasses, the rub density on primary points was 4.4. It was 5.2 on secondary land-points.

We dragged clipboards and reels of measuring tape everywhere we went, even when we crawled through 100 yards of a nearly impenetrable

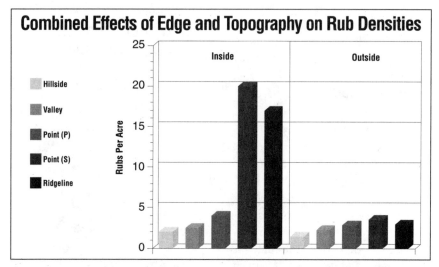

Combined Effects of Edge and Topography on Rub Densities

The effects of habitat edges and topography on rub distribution are cumulative. If a soft edge occurs along a ridgeline, for example, it's even more attractive to traveling bucks. Therefore, bucks are more likely to use an edge as a travel corridor when it runs along a ridgeline or secondary point. Rub densities inside edge zones were five times greater when the edges were on secondary points and ridges, rather than in valleys or on hillsides. This chart shows how rub densities inside edge zones compared to rub densities in topography outside edge zones. As you can see, the combined qualities of edge and topography definitely attract traveling deer.

10-year-old clearcuts to check every sapling within a 10-meter radius of the transit line. The project was a lot of work. Sometimes we walked and sometimes we crawled to thoroughly check more than two miles of transit lines. But the knowledge we gained from the data was worth it.

Our Results

As expected, rub distributions were affected by edge types, but that influence only extended about 10 meters. We did not find significantly higher rub densities past the 10-meter boundary.

Surprisingly, though, the edge types that affected rub distribution the most were "soft" edges. The soft edges were created by subtle changes in forest or cover type, especially where mature forests met younger growth to produce the highest edge effect. We had expected to see more influence from "hard" edges, such as field edges or powerline right-of-ways.

Creeks also produced an increase in rub density. However, contrary to some theories we read about, creeks were the least influential edge type.

Because edges exert a strong 10-meter influence, we separated data

In reviewing our records, we found 70 percent of the mature bucks we killed were taken from secondary points that descended from a ridgetop.

from the land-use and topography zones for more analysis. By removing these data from the calculations, the influence of land-use and topography was isolated from the edge effects. With the edge data removed, we discovered that land-use classifications had little influence on rub density.

The Influence of Topography

Because the landscapes were similar across the study area, they might have altered our findings. But what can't be denied is the influence that topography had on rub distribution. Rub densities per acre for the different topographic features were:

✓ Ridgelines, 4.7,

✓ Points, 4.5,

✓ Valleys, 3.7,

✓ Hillsides, 1.9.

We broke the points down into two subclasses for more analysis. The rub densities on these subclasses were:

✓ Primary points, 4.4,

✓ Secondary points, 5.2.

Although topography wasn't as influential on rub location as edges, the numbers confirmed our suspicions that rubs are more prevalent on ridges and points than in valleys or on hillsides.

Why did secondary points have a higher rub density than primary points? We don't know for sure, but these findings matched our earlier scouting reports, which found that most active rub lines ran along ridgelines, and up and down secondary points.

Without fully realizing it, our group had been taking advantage of these ridgeline and secondary-point travel corridors for some time. In reviewing our records, we found that 70 percent of the mature bucks we killed were taken from secondary points that descended from a ridgetop.

We also confirmed that bucks and does use ridgelines as main travel corridors. In the survey area, bucks used secondary points as entrance and exit "ramps" to and from ridges. That's probably because the gradual ascent of secondary points allow the easiest access to the ridgetops.

We also found the highest concentration of scrapes at intersections of

> *The highest concentration of scrapes are at intersections of ridgelines and secondary points. By making rubs near an 'entrance ramp' onto a deer highway, bucks get maximum exposure.*

ridgelines and secondary points. That makes sense because scrapes are a form of signpost communication between deer. By placing rubs near an entrance ramp onto a deer highway, bucks ensure the rubs get maximum exposure.

After re-examining our rub maps, we noticed another pattern. Bucks, as the breeding season approaches, expand their range by moving one entrance or exit ramp farther down a ridgeline. By the time peak activity occurs, a buck might have expanded its range several miles down a ridgeline by using six or more secondary points.

A final conclusion from our survey is probably the most important clue to locating rub lines in any land-use situation: The effects of edges and topography on rub distribution are cumulative. If a soft edge occurs along a ridgeline, for example, it's even more attractive to traveling deer.

In one ridge-line/secondary point intersection we studied, two types of soft edges converged. In this area, we found more than 100 rubs per acre. This was true for all edges, not just soft edges. Field edges, powerline right-of-ways, and even old logging roads were enhanced when they lay along favorable topography.

Rubs in edge zones were five times as frequent when the edges were on ridges and secondary points. Therefore, bucks are more likely to use an edge as a travel corridor when it runs along a ridge or secondary point.

Conclusion

Because edges have a strong effect on rub lines, it's easiest to find them in farm country by following terrain funnels, field edges and fencerows. Also, take note of prominent topography, especially ridges and points.

If you hunt in big timber, look for more subtle influences on deer movement. In our study, soft edges formed by transitions in forest species or their age and size played an important role in buck-travel patterns and rub-line locations. Regardless of land use, you must factor in the influence of topography in your mental equations.

Remember, deer tend to use ridgelines as highways. Use a topographic map and your knowledge of the terrain to locate the subtle ramps onto and off of these corridors. From there, get out on foot and look for ramps and corridors that also have good edge habitat.

As the breeding activity peaks, bucks seek areas with high concentrations of does. Therefore, these intersections are prime sites for bucks to interact with multiple doe groups while providing maximum exposure for buck signposts.

We noticed that the hottest buck and estrous-doe activity occurs during the peak of the rut near ridges and secondary point intersections. In fact, throughout the breeding cycle, these intersections produced the earliest and most consistent buck signpost activity.

Greg's Practical Points

➤ *The hottest buck and estrous doe activity occurs during the peak of the rut near ridges and secondary point intersections.*

➤ *The effects of edges and topography on rub distribution are cumulative. If a soft edge occurs along a ridgeline, for example, it's even more attractive to traveling deer.*

➤ *Predicting where bucks will show up requires more than locating a few rubs and studying topographical maps. Hunters need to understand how terrain, cover and edge effect work together to concentrate deer movement.*

➤ *Some of the busiest rub sites were junctions of ridgelines and points with "soft" cover edges. "Soft" edges are subtle changes in forest or cover type within the woods, especially where mature forests meet younger growth to produce the highest edge effect.*

This 1985 photo shows me with my brother Jeff after we located a large rub on a good-sized balsam fir. We found the rub while scouting in the spring. Off-season scouting wasn't as common 20 to 30 years ago as it is today. Many serious deer hunters now hit the woods year-round to stay abreast of deer in their favorite areas.

Chapter 5

AN EXPLANATION
OF RUB LINES

The information in preceding chapters is extremely important, and it provides the foundation for what lies ahead in this book. Whether you're an ascending hunter or a well-established trophy-buck hunter, you must have the knowledge base we laid down in the first four chapters. Without that foundation, your success rate won't improve much.

I chuckle when I think back to the early stages of my rub-line hunting days. Once I realized rubs could be used as scouting and hunting aids for big bucks, I became possessed. I hit the woods at every opportunity. My job as a seasonal construction worker provided the luxury of scouting for weeks during the off-season. Of course, off-season scouting is now a common practice among deer hunters, but I assure you few were doing it in the late 1970s and early '80s. In fact, it wasn't until the latter part of the 1980s that I saw many hunters interested in it.

Don't confuse the terminology I use in this book. When I say rub lines, I'm not referring to scrape lines, as some readers might assume. Contrary to what you might think, rub lines and scrape lines aren't always found along the same travel corridors. Although they will sometimes follow the same path, this generally isn't the rule.

In any event, I stress again that you can't become an effective rub-line hunter until you possess hard-earned knowledge about all aspects of rub behavior. It's crucial you know why bucks rub, how they relate to their rubs throughout the season, how to accurately read individual rubs, and where and why rubs are concentrated in certain areas. Once you have a strong grasp of all those intricate details, and you develop a solid understanding of the things I'll cover in this chapter, all the remaining pieces of the rub-line puzzle will naturally fall into place. And remember, you must take this book information and apply it in the field while scouting and hunting.

A simple explanation of a rub line is a series (line) of rubs made along the most preferred travel routes of white-tailed bucks.

What Exactly are Rub Lines?

That subhead might sound basic to some deer hunters, but I want to define rub lines in exact detail. Hunters occasionally tell me how much they love to hunt big bucks along rub lines. However, when I ask some detailed questions about their experiences, it becomes apparent they don't know the first thing about rub lines. Heck, most of them don't even know what a rub line really is.

Let's set our definitions. Rub lines aren't a concentration of three or four rubs in a small area. And when I talk about rub lines, I'm not referring to scrapes. For reasons that mystify me, some hunters confuse rub lines with scrape lines. Maybe they presume I'm guilty of misspeaking; that I really mean to say "scrape line" instead of "rub line." Some have even asked if I meant to say "scrape line." No, you heard right.

This confusion isn't nearly as common as it was when I started preaching my rub-line beliefs. However, I still see enough confusion of the terms to warrant mention. Besides, it provides a perfect lead-in to help me clearly define rub lines.

Contrary to what some hunters believe, rub lines and scrape lines aren't always laid out through the same travel corridors. Please note that I didn't say rubs and scrapes weren't always found in the same places. I said rub lines and scrape lines weren't always in the same corridors. Sometimes they are, but most times scrape lines follow different corridors than rub lines. Why big bucks prefer to do this requires far too much speculation.

You probably noticed I mentioned corridors several times in the previous paragraph. Travel corridors, at least the preferred travel corridors of big bucks, are a tip-off in locating most rub lines. A simple explanation of a rub line is a series (line) of rubs made along the most preferred travel routes of white-tailed bucks.

While rub lines aren't a straight line, they connect a definite Point A to a definite Point B. In other words, when traveling about their ranges, non-rutting bucks almost always follow one of their rub lines. And, by the way, a buck's rub lines appear along his morning and afternoon travel routes.

I've long believed that scrapes have little or nothing to do with buck-doe interactions. Scrapes, I believe, are mostly a "buck thing," in much the same way that fire hydrants are of far more interest to male dogs than female dogs. If a buck meets a doe with the help of a scrape, it's a freak occurrence.

Scrapes are a Buck Thing

Although rubs and rub lines play a huge role in the daily lives of bucks, this aspect of buck behavior has received little attention from hunters or the scientific community. That's likely because everyone seemed focused on scrapes. Many of the scrape "insights" assumed that scraping provides bucks with their sole means of scent-marking/scent-checking their territories. Many people also assumed that bucks establish scrapes to attract and meet potential mates. For years we were force-fed this notion that scrapes were a buck-doe thing.

My experience is that scrapes are mainly a "buck thing." Does no doubt happen upon them at times and may even check one occasionally out of curiosity, but I will never believe that scrapes somehow act as a bulletin board or dating service to bring "single, willing" deer together. If you've read my first book, *Aggressive Whitetail Hunting*, attended my seminars, or read my magazine articles regularly, you know bucks tend to use scrapes in much the same manner that male dogs use fire hydrants. They mostly just let each other know who's in the neighborhood.

That's a far different, less systematic purpose than what is found in rubs. Most rub lines identify a buck's preferred travel routes through his home range. Bucks start rubbing the minute they shed their velvet, and they continue to make new rubs almost daily. They also rework and freshen some rubs almost daily.

Why do bucks rub so much? Well, just consider what we've already

Bucks rub trees, saplings and brush for many reasons. Besides rubbing to rid themselves of velvet, build their neck muscles and show aggression toward other bucks, male whitetails rub for much the same reason they make scrapes: to advertise their presence and to keep tabs on other bucks in their area.

covered. Yes, bucks rub to remove some of their velvet. They also rub to help build up and strengthen their neck muscles. They also rub to show aggression and intimidate other bucks.

But bucks make rubs and rub lines for far more reasons than those. Although it wasn't widely known until recently, rubs serve much the same purpose as scrapes. Like scrapes, rubs are made in places frequented most often by other bucks.

And also like scrapes, mature bucks use rubs to keep track of other buck activity in their core areas throughout the lengthy pre-rut, and to continually announce their own presence to other bucks that venture past these odorous signposts. Just as they do with scrapes, bucks saturate rubs

Some rub concentrations appear in the woods for no apparent reason. I believe some of these sites pinpoint where neighboring bucks "trespass" onto another buck's core area. If you find a site where a buck is in the habit of testing another's boundary, it's probably worth your time in the final days of the pre-rut to hang a stand and wait for one of the antagonists to return.

with their scent. Each buck that visits an active rub will know with a sniff if other bucks have visited that rub in the past 24 to 36 hours.

The Role of Scent

It's important to understand the large role that scent plays in rub communication. I'll share a story to explain my point. My brother Jeff and I once bow-hunted a 290-acre chunk of farmland near our homes. A bachelor group of six bucks was living on the property one season. One buck was a real whopper, two were solid shooters, and the other three were immature bucks. With so many bucks in the area, rubbing activity on the farm was nearly unbelievable. While we continually found fresh rubs across the acreage, a couple of spots in particular held concentrated rub activity. We couldn't figure out why until the latter stages of the pre-rut.

On two occasions while bow-hunting in late October, I saw a big buck

*Depending on the area, I believe 80 percent
to 90 percent of rub lines link primary
feeding areas with preferred bedding areas.*

waltz onto our property near one of the spots that was extremely rubbed up. Each time, the buck walked right over and sniffed a few of the rubs. He then spent several minutes rubbing, licking and, in general, thoroughly scent-marking one or two rubs. Afterward he stood around like he was waiting for one of the resident bucks to appear. Both times I saw him, he didn't go any farther onto the property. That changed once the rut kicked into gear. Jeff and I then saw him cruising our farm in November.

While most rub lines are made along a buck's preferred travel routes, I've also noticed that some mature bucks often rub in spots that aren't preferred travel corridors. I think they have one reason for doing this: Resident big bucks know that if they have "trespass problems" with "neighboring" big bucks, the encroachment will likely occur in these spots. I've found these sometimes isolated rub concentrations are effective sites for ambushing mature bucks, especially during the final week of the pre-rut.

Links to Other Big Bucks

Let's explore that behavior a little further. Depending on the area, I believe 80 percent to 90 percent of rub lines link primary feeding areas with preferred bedding areas. Also, depending on location, I estimate 5 percent to 10 percent of all rub lines link bedding areas with water sources. The remaining percentage of rub lines link a buck's bedding areas with "miscellaneous" spots other than food or water. While "no-goal-in-sight" rub lines are rare, it's important to know where to find and understand them. At a certain time during the season, hunting these rub lines can be productive.

These miscellaneous rub lines often link the core areas of some big bucks with the core areas of other big bucks. Mature white-tailed bucks constantly test the core-area perimeters of other big bucks. I liken this to the boundary-testing that goes on between hostile countries. Earlier in my life, I was in the intelligence division of the U.S. Air Force. During my 18 months in Alaska, I monitored activities at several Russian air bases in Siberia. We were constantly tracking fighters and bombers that

---

Rub lines can reveal how a buck approaches, enters or leaves preferred areas. I can study a rub line and learn within inches where a buck likes to walk.

---

took off from those bases, flew across the Bering Sea, and tested the perimeters of our so-called "defense lines." Of course, U.S. aircraft constantly tested the perimeters of Russia's defense lines, too. It just seemed a big game.

From what I've seen, big bucks enjoy playing a similar game occasionally. They also seem to enjoy leaving unmistakable evidence that they invaded another buck's home turf. Still, I don't think it's a common practice. I've found that rub lines linking the core areas of big bucks tend to have far fewer rubs than rub lines linking bedding areas to feeding areas. That's because, for most of the fall, travel routes between feeding and bedding areas get far more use than any other travel routes. That changes during the final days of the pre-rut. At this time, big bucks spend enormous amounts of time and energy testing the defense lines of other big bucks.

I don't need to explain where some of your late pre-rut hunting efforts should be concentrated!

What Rub Lines Can Tell Us About Buck Movements

One reason I have so much faith in rub lines is because they can reveal so much about how a buck approaches, enters or leaves its preferred areas. I can study a rub line and figure out within inches where a big buck likes to walk.

And where do most big bucks prefer to walk? Man, I could play a lot more golf if I had a dollar for every time I've been asked that question. Each big buck seems to have his own quirks and preferences when establishing travel routes. Some bucks seem content to travel the exact same corridors and rub in almost the identical places as their predecessors. Other bucks make rub lines along corridors where I've never seen other deer walk. About the only thing most rub lines have in common is that they're established along routes where bucks can use the terrain to their full advantage. In some cases, their rub lines follow routes that give the bucks great visibility. In other cases, the bucks can use their sense of smell to its full extent. And in yet other cases, rub lines are near the area's thickest cover. At any hint of danger, a buck traveling these rub

Bucks sometimes like to test the "defense lines" of another buck's territory. Still, I don't think this is an everyday occurrence. Bucks travel the routes between bedding and feeding areas far more often than they follow routes to another buck's core area. As a result, more rubs are found along the bucks' bedding-feeding routes than along routes going elsewhere.

Big bucks don't always restrict their travel to thick cover. I estimate that about half the rub lines I find are in fairly open cover. When setting up on any rub line, take precautions to ensure you won't be easily spotted. Big bucks trust their eyesight to detect danger far more than many hunters believe.

lines can bound once or twice and be swallowed up by thick cover.

Let's also clear up a misconception regarding where most rub lines are located. Contrary to what many hunters believe, big bucks don't restrict their travel to an area's thickest, most impenetrable cover. In fact, of the hundreds of big-buck rub lines I've scouted the past 20 years, at least half went through rather open forests or woods. I know some of those rub lines were strictly nocturnal travel corridors, but I believe just as many were used for some daytime big-buck travel.

I've also learned that, while bucks most prefer to use their noses, mature bucks greatly trust their eyesight to warn them of danger. If you're reluctant to believe that fact, you'll struggle to achieve consistent success on large-racked deer. Why? If you don't heavily consider the buck's eyesight, you'll overlook many potentially productive stand sites, or you'll set up where a buck will easily see you.

Greg's Practical Points ————————

➤ *Rub lines aren't a concentration of three or four rubs in a small area.*

➤ *A rub line is a series of rubs made along the most preferred travel routes of white-tailed bucks. While rub lines aren't a straight line, they connect a definite Point A to a definite Point B.*

➤ *Rub lines appear along a buck's morning and afternoon travel routes.*

➤ *Mature bucks use rubs to keep track of other buck activity in their core areas throughout the lengthy pre-rut. Rubs continually announce a buck's presence to other bucks that venture past these odorous signposts.*

➤ *Most rub lines connect bedding and feeding areas, and a few link bedding sites to water sources. Less common are rub lines linking core areas of some big bucks with the core areas of other big bucks.*

➤ *About half of all rub lines occur in fairly open forests or woods. While some of those rub lines are strictly nocturnal travel corridors, just as many are used for some daytime big-buck travel.*

➤ *Mature bucks greatly trust their eyesight to warn them of danger. If you're reluctant to believe that fact, you'll struggle to achieve consistent success on large-racked deer.*

If you think bucks are easily patterned, chances are you're thinking in broad, general terms. There's a big difference between knowing that a buck moves daily between bedding and feeding areas, and pinpointing a precise spot to waylay him with a bullet or arrow. Figuring out the buck's preferred food source is only one piece of the puzzle.

Chapter 6

SCOUTING AND UNRAVELING RUB LINES

I've often heard hunters say white-tailed bucks aren't that difficult to pattern. They believe a buck's daily travel routines are dictated exclusively by his preferred food sources. Supposedly, a buck travels from his bedding area to the primary food source in the late afternoon/early evening. He then spends most of the night pigging out. At some point in the early morning, he starts heading back to his bedding area. By first light, he's near or already safely bedded in his hideout.

That sounds like a simple pattern to figure out, right? I've always said it doesn't take a brain surgeon to figure out the whitetail's basic movement patterns. However, there's a world of difference between learning general daily movements and knowing exactly where a buck

While individual rubs are interesting in their own right, they don't tell me much about a buck's preferred travel routes. It's important to find rubs that are part of an actual rub line, and then piece together the pieces of these fascinating puzzles as they snake their way through a woods or forest. Once that task is accomplished, I can start figuring out where the buck will take his next step.

will walk when employing those patterns. If my observations of deer hunters are any indication, many don't have a clue about pinpointing a buck's preferred travel routes. And let's face it: It's darned hard to ambush a big buck if you have no idea where he is walking when he travels about his home range. I struggled big time with this problem in my early years of trophy hunting.

Rub Lines Solve Buck Riddles

About 20 years ago, I hit on a system for figuring out where big bucks prefer to walk. Although I knew my system was the most reliable way to pinpoint buck routes, I didn't share it. At least not right away. It's not that I was selfish or afraid of teaching other hunters a key to my success. Actually, I assumed most successful deer hunters already knew the importance of using rubs and rub lines when hunting mature bucks. As I eventually discovered, however, few knew the significance of rubs and even fewer knew anything about rub lines.

But I also knew my own rub and rub-line education was just beginning! My infatuation with rubs and rub lines was a blessing. Not only did it make me a productive hunter, it also led me to my career

Although I knew rub lines were the most reliable way to pinpoint buck travel routes, I didn't share the secret. I assumed most successful deer hunters already knew the significance of rub lines.

as a full-time free-lance photographer and outdoor writer. My understanding of rub lines also played a big role in turning me into a deer hunting educator and seminar speaker.

One of the first things I discovered is that one rub seldom provides enough insights into a buck's habits. About the only way to learn a buck's travel routes is to identify potential rub lines and then piece them together.

A Buck's Typical Routine

To effectively scout for rub lines, I'll first illustrate the typical routine of a mature buck each evening during the lengthy pre-rut period. (Of course, this is the routine of an undisturbed deer.) When a buck rises from his bed, he first stretches and then stands almost motionless a few minutes. All the while he is looking, smelling and listening to see if he can detect nearby threats.

After assuring himself everything is normal, the buck moves a short distance and relieves himself. When he's finished, he again checks for threats. Once the buck believes he's safe, he'll rub small trees or bushes for a few minutes. He then gets on a runway that leads to his destination. All along this route, the buck leaves evidence of his passing. This evidence is rubs. The buck will also make rubs all the way back to this bedding area in the morning.

This routine points out where most rub lines are located: between a buck's preferred bedding and feeding areas. Almost all of my rub-line scouting begins near feeding areas. In farmlands, I key on standard agricultural attractants, like alfalfa, corn and soybean fields. In the big woods and forests, almost all of my scouting begins near large browse areas, which are almost always 1- to 5-year-old clearcuts. I also scout intensely around stands of oaks in the big woods. Oaks, of course, are cyclical in acorn production, so they don't produce a good crop every year. I always scout the oaks every spring so I'll be a jump ahead should they be a hot ticket in the fall.

When a buck rises from his bed to prepare for a feeding foray, he first stretches and then stands almost motionless a few minutes. All the while he is looking, smelling and listening for any hints of danger. After that, he moves off a short distance to relieve himself. After again checking for danger, he hits the trail.

I've found 1- to 5-year-old clear-cuts to be excellent sources of food for forest and big-woods whitetails. The new growth in clear-cuts provides browse that tastes like candy to whitetails. I walk the perimeter of clear-cuts, trying to find rub lines that indicate a buck's preferred entry or exit sites to this food source.

Prime Scouting Times

The post-season and spring are the best times to scout for rub lines. Visibility in the woods is never better than these two times, and visibility is a critical factor for scouting rub lines. The other reason I prefer to scout for rub lines during the spring and post-season is the "disturbance factor." At these times, I can scout rub lines in their entirety — from food sources to bedding areas — without worrying

A deer trail of some sort will almost always link rubs in a rub line. Isolated rubs with no obvious trail nearby seldom will be part of a rub line. Isolated concentrations of rubs are usually just that: isolated. Sure, there will always be exceptions. But 20 years of rub-line experience tells me that runways are the vital link to defining and scouting a buck's rub lines.

After I pinpoint a preferred feeding area, I walk its perimeter looking for rubs. I pay the most attention to wrist-sized and larger rubs, and try to determine if they're part of an actual rub line.

if I'll hurt my chances on future hunts. And because a buck's rub lines appear pretty much along the same routes each year, things you find in the off-season will likely be duplicated in the fall.

So, let's get moving. After I pinpoint a preferred feeding area, I walk its perimeter looking for rubs. While I check each rub I find, I pay the most attention to wrist-sized and larger rubs. When finding such rubs, I try to determine if they're an isolated concentration or part of an actual rub line. Isolated concentrations of buck sign are just that — isolated!

I seldom find runways leading to such sign. It's almost as if the rub(s) is made purely at random. On the other hand, I almost always find a runway of some sort alongside rubs that are part of a rub line. I realize this sounds ridiculously simple, but 20 years worth of experience have proven it's reliable.

Once I locate a rub line, I determine if it's a morning or evening travel route by studying the direction the rubs are facing. If the rubs consistently face the feeding area (meaning you can see them from the feeding area), the rub line is a morning route. The buck is rubbing as he leaves the feeding area.

If the rubs face away from the feeding area, it's an evening route. The buck is rubbing as he approaches the feeding area. Remember that rubs always face away from the direction the buck is traveling. Never forget that when you're trying to unravel difficult rub lines.

Seeking the Source

I always try to follow morning rub lines all the way from a feeding area to the buck's bedding area. While I follow rub lines, I constantly turn around and scan the woods behind me to look for rubs that face away from the bedding area. Those rubs might be part of an evening rub line. So, even though I begin by scouting a morning rub line, I quickly start paying attention for evening rub lines, too.

When I spot rubs that are likely part of an evening rub-line, I mentally note their location and continue scouting the morning rub

After tracing a morning rub line back to a buck's bedding area, I try to locate evening rub lines that lead away from the bedding area. I seldom hunt the midsections of a rub line. I find it's better to have some good stand sites picked out at the beginning and end of the rub lines.

Too many hunters think rub lines will be as obvious as a bug on their partner's nose. If unraveling rub lines were that easy, a lot more monster bucks would be killed each year!

line. If I succeed in tracing the rub line back to the bedding area, I study the lay of the land. After familiarizing myself with the topography, I look for the start of evening rub lines. In those rare cases when I can't find the beginning of an evening rub-line near a bedding area, I return to the suspected evening rubs I spotted earlier. I then start scouting at that point.

Even though most rub lines link bedding and feeding areas, it often pays to find rub lines that lead to water sources. This is especially important when hunting big bucks in the early season. It's even more important should you be hunting in extremely dry conditions. Big bucks — and all whitetails, for that matter — need water daily throughout fall, including the rut.

Unraveling Rub Lines

Unraveling a rub line can be difficult for any hunter. In fact, I answer more questions about this task than any other aspect of rub-line hunting. After talking with many hunters, it's obvious too many of them think rub lines will be as obvious as a bug on their partner's nose. If unraveling rub lines were as easy as strolling from rub to rub, there would be one heck of a lot more monster bucks killed each year!

Of the hundreds of rub lines I've scouted, only a handful were relatively easy to unravel. Most took a lot of time and tremendous effort to figure out. And a fair number, try as I might, forever baffled me. Some bucks travel in such unpredictable and totally irrational ways (in my opinion, anyway) that it's virtually impossible to figure out their next step. This doesn't mean, however, that tough rub lines are always impossible to unravel. It just means it will take more time, effort and possibly luck to complete the job.

I've found topographical maps invaluable, and I like to carry them with me as I scout for and unravel rub lines. When I find the beginnings of a rub line, I check the map to see if I can correlate the location of those rubs with a possible bedding area. I don't use the maps

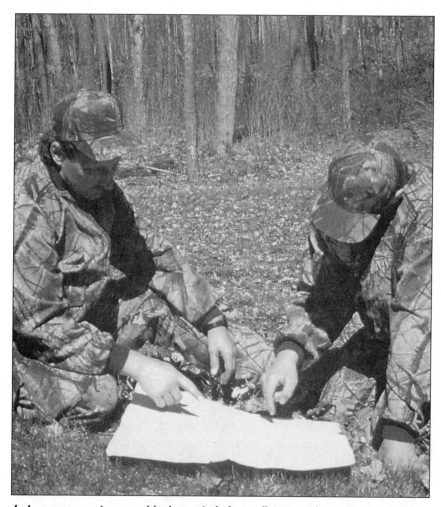

I always carry a topographical map to help me figure out how a buck might use the terrain. I don't use the map as a substitute for leg work. However, wise use of a topo map can help me scout and hunt more efficiently. I once used a map to pinpoint a buck's possible bedding area. The map showed a swamp about 600 yards away from some rubs I had found. Because most of the area was clear-cut, I knew the swamp was one of the few places a buck could bed.

to do less leg work. I use them to understand the topography, which helps immensely for locating the next rub in a line. In fact, I can sometimes study a topo map to figure out where a rub line will likely be found, and then pinpoint it by studying the immediate surroundings. As many successful trophy hunters can attest, undisturbed whitetails usually travel woodland routes that allow the easiest

Bucks almost always will display some regional preferences in their travel routes. I've found that bucks in big woods or forests like to make rub lines along the edges of swamps. Farmland whitetails relate to thick brush lines that connect woodlots. And Canadian bucks often like to make rub lines through thick stands of poplar or along the edges of red willow/swamp grass swales that bisect large wheat fields.

passage.

I don't know about other hunters, but I often pinpoint these passages simply by letting my instincts or experience take over. For instance, I learned long ago that instead of crossing hilltops just anywhere, whitetails prefer to cross in slight depressions or saddles. I also know big bucks especially like to travel through points of

Overnight, big bucks seem to go from being reclusive and daylight-shy to obvious and active in daylight. I then switch from stands near bedding areas to stands near feeding areas.

cover. Many big-woods rub lines I've hunted ran along swamp edges. It's also a fact that monster farmland bucks relate big time to thick brush lines that connect woodlots. And Canadian bucks love to make rub lines through thick poplar stands and along the edges of red willow/swamp grass swales that often bisect large wheat fields.

In fact, bucks display definite regional patterns when making rub lines. This can be another key factor in unraveling a rub-line.

Know When to Quit Searching

While it's sometimes important to unravel rub lines in their entirety, it's not always a requirement. These days, I completely unravel only about half of the rub lines I hunt. Why? I seldom hunt the midsections of rub lines. I usually set up near a buck's bedding area or, as the rut nears, close to feeding areas. I've found that, overnight, big bucks seem to go from being reclusive and daylight-shy to obvious and active in daylight. Because of that, I quickly switch from stands near bedding areas to stands near feeding areas. That's why there's no need to explore or even locate a rub line's midsection.

Wisconsin's firearms deer season provided an experience that perfectly illustrates that point. I was scouting near the edge of a 5-year-old clearcut when I found a couple of active rub lines. I immediately pulled out my topo map. Rather than trying to figure out where the big buck was walking, I tried to figure out where he was bedding. This turned out to be relatively easy. The map showed a small swamp about 600 yards back from the clearcut. Although small, the swamp provided the area's only suitable bedding habitat. I hiked to the swamp and, along its edge, found several rubs on fairly large trees. I also found a short line of rubs going away from the swamp. This obviously was one of the buck's evening routes! After looking around some more, I found part of a morning rub line. From this sign, I figured that most of the buck's daytime activities occurred near the swamp, so I followed each rub line only about 75 yards. I picked out a couple of potential stand sites and then left. I ambushed

I killed this buck in 1986 after finding and hunting only one part of his rub line. While I like to scout an entire rub line and find its definite beginning and end, that simply isn't possible in all cases. If I find a place along a rub line where I'm confident the buck is spending some time in daylight, I don't hesitate to pick a couple of good stand sites and get ready to hunt.

My rub-line hunting success hasn't suffered since I've become less concerned with scouting every inch of every rub line beginning to end. I'm not as concerned with a rub line's midsection.

the buck along the evening rub line late on the fourth day of the gun season.

Granted, things don't always go that smoothly, but I've found just enough success to keep me setting up along active rub lines. Also, my rub-line success hasn't suffered since I've become less concerned with scouting each rub line beginning to end. That doesn't mean I don't try to thoroughly scout every rub line. I just don't make it the priority I once did. This is especially true when I scout rub lines during the fall, and don't want to risk disturbing the buck.

Some Final Words

One last thing. While topo maps, aerial photos and other aids can help you unravel rub lines, don't forsake some common sense. Don't make deer hunting more difficult than it already is by overlooking and/or ignoring the obvious. I know one guy who for several years refused to hunt certain rub lines because he couldn't visualize a big ol' buck walking through those spots. He believed the spots just weren't thick enough! Well, maybe the cover wasn't thick enough for his tastes, but there was something about these sites that big bucks liked.

Bottom line? If all signs indicate a big deer is regularly using a corridor, hunt that deer right there! Don't continually out-think yourself into hunting the wrong spots.

I'm certainly not the most knowledgeable or successful big-buck hunter in the world. By the same token, I've had fairly good success on mature bucks the past 20 years by scouting and unraveling their rub lines. It hasn't hurt that I try to apply common sense to each situation.

Greg's Practical Points

➤ One rub seldom provides enough insights into a buck's habits. About the only way to learn a buck's travel routes is by identifying potential rub lines and then piecing them together.

➤ Post-season and spring are the best times to scout for rub lines. Visibility in the woods is never better, and you don't have to worry if you disturb bucks when invading their bedding areas.

➤ Runways seldom accompany "isolated" buck rubs. Such rubs are made at random. A runway of some sort will almost always follow rubs that are part of a rub line.

➤ Start scouting by walking the perimeter of feeding areas. Pay the most attention to wrist-sized and larger rubs. Determine if they're random rubs or part of a rub line.

➤ Morning rub lines are identified by rubs that face the feeding area. That is, you can see them from the feeding area. A buck made the rubs as it departed the feeding area. Evening rub lines are identified by rubs that face away from the feeding area. They were made as the buck approached the feeding area.

➤ While it's sometimes important to unravel rub lines in their entirety, I completely unravel only about half of them. Why? I seldom hunt a rub line's midsection.

➤ If all signs indicate a big deer is regularly using a corridor, hunt that deer right there! Don't continually out-think yourself into hunting the wrong spots.

Many hunters mistakenly believe hunting is equally good along any of a buck's rub lines. Because not all rub lines are created equal, deer hunters must thoroughly scout each rub line to learn which ones are a buck's preferred travel routes.

Chapter 7

CHOOSING KILLER STAND SITES

Finding active rub lines does not guarantee big-buck success. I spent several years struggling with the rub-line/stand-placement challenge before discovering an important fact: Forests and deer woods hold far more unproductive than productive rub-line stand sites.

This is a major stumbling block for deer hunters, no matter their depth of experience, and I think I know why. When trying to pick killer stand sites, too many hunters believe all rub lines are created equal. When scouting and hunting a buck's various rub lines, realize the productivity of one rub line will never be the same as another's.

Finding productive rub-line stands involves more than just locating the most active rub lines. You must locate a specific productive site along the rub line. Believe it or not, this might mean guessing, almost to the yard, where some daylight buck activity will occur.

Making this task even more difficult is that each big buck has a unique

I've refined my approach for finding productive stands along rub lines. No matter what the buck's temperament, my way of picking stand sites along rub lines will often put me in position for a shot at bucks like the one shown here. If you're seeking a shortcut, I'll disappoint you. It requires a lot of work.

temperament. I've refined my approach for finding rub-line stand sites. With the exception of bucks that are totally nocturnal in their movements, my system has proven deadly on every other type of whitetail personality. To master this system, you must pay some dues. Even if you consider yourself a natural at deer hunting, you must bust your hump to achieve even modest success at hunting rub-line bucks.

Post-Season Scouting for Stand Sites

Not surprisingly, picking the right stands begins with post-season scouting. I have always loved scouting at this time of year. The hunting seasons are over, and the woods are mostly void of humans. You can pretty much be assured mature bucks have returned to core areas

My brother Mike and I found this rub line while post-season scouting. I think the post-season is the best time of all to scout for productive rub lines and stand sites. By this time of the year, many bucks will have reverted to using their pre-rut travel routes and bedding areas.

they used during the pre-rut. They will also be using many of their pre-rut travel routes.

Most importantly, though, is that most bucks will still be carrying their antlers. As long as they have antlers, they'll do some rubbing. Fresh rubs and reworked rubs can tell you exactly which rub lines the bucks prefer. Your job isn't over, however. Once you figure out which rub lines produce the most buck activity, you must find out exactly where to place your stands along those rub lines.

Before continuing, I must stress again that it's possible to select good rub-line stands nearly a year in advance. I'm often asked if bucks will establish their rub lines along the same routes in fall. There's no rule ensuring this will always happen, but it occurs often enough for me to pick stand sites in the off-season.

Mature bucks display many of the same tendencies toward rubbing as they

Just as they tend to do with scrapes, white-tailed bucks often rub in the same places year after year. This tree has been rubbed for at least three consecutive years. It's not unusual for several generations of bucks to rub the same trees or trees nearby along the same travel route.

do scraping. As you no doubt know, bucks often scrape in the same spots each year. The same goes for rubbing, because, as with scrapes, bucks use rubs to help monitor buck activity in their core areas. In fact, I'm sure most deer hunters have found trees that were rubbed several years in a row.

Also like scraping, bucks tend to rub in specific spots and along certain routes from one generation to the next. That's why information gleaned from post-season scouting can be beneficial for many hunting seasons. I've hunted some rub lines more than 10 years, and I know dozens of hunters who can make the same claim.

Of course, we're not always hunting the same deer that first got our attention. But that doesn't matter. Bucks like certain travel routes for a reason, and

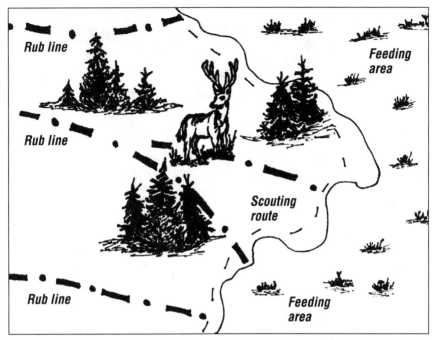

I begin many of my rub-line scouting trips by walking around the outside edge of deer feeding areas. This is a great way to find one end of a rub line.

barring a dramatic change in the habitat or landscape, they'll continue using them indefinitely.

I found one of my most productive morning rub-line stands during a post-season scouting trip. This rub line linked a nighttime feeding area to a bedding area. After studying the situation, I picked a stand site in a large white oak about 75 yards from the bedding area. After a couple of sits during the open season, I realized I was slightly out of position. I made the necessary adjustments, and then enjoyed a string of eight successful, memorable seasons. My partners and I killed some good bucks in that time, and we saw a bunch more. Unfortunately, a rude hunter moved in and ruined the spot.

Finding the Right Spots

Let's discuss how to find the most productive stand sites. This is where the work starts. It's often no great shakes to scout one or two big-buck rub lines. It's far more difficult to scout almost every rub line a buck makes.

You might think it's unnecessary to scout every one of a buck's rub lines. But remember, this chapter's title is "Choosing Killer Stand Sites." That means finding sites with the most potential in each area. In many cases you

It's crucial to know where the deer you're hunting likes to bed. If you don't have this vital information, it's difficult to know how closely you can place your tree stand to a buck's bedding area. The post-season allows you to intrude into a buck's bedding area without worrying about making him feel pressured.

When choosing stand sites near a buck's bedding area, make sure you are far enough away from his hideouts to allow you to enter and leave your stand without alerting him to your presence. If you did your homework in the post-season, you circled the bedding area and located the buck's preferred entry and exit routes.

won't find these places unless you first eliminate all other potential sites. There is no shortcut in this process of elimination. You must personally check out each and every possibility.

As you'll recall from the previous chapter, it's imperative to locate the end of rub lines near bedding areas. The post-season is one of the rare times it's OK to walk in and explore a buck's bedding areas. In fact, once you pinpoint the bedding area "ends" of rub lines, you really should walk into the buck's bedroom. By walking around in the bedding areas, you can learn how a buck prefers to enter and leave his daytime hideouts. This information is invaluable when trying to locate the most productive rub-line stand sites.

While it's possible to trick a buck's hearing or vision, it's nearly impossible to consistently beat his sense of smell. For this reason, it's imperative to have several stand sites prepared in advance for every conceivable wind condition. Whenever possible, take care of this requirement during the off-season.

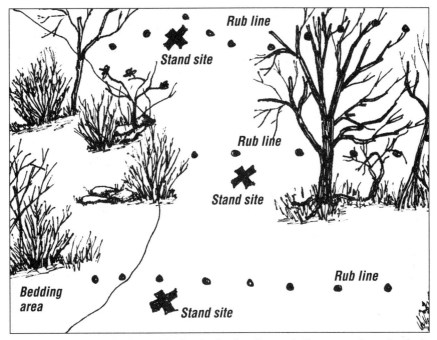

Rub line

Stand site

Rub line

Stand site

Rub line

Bedding
area

Stand site

I've had my best luck on big bucks by hunting rub lines as close to their bedding areas as possible. This "rule" applies for most of the fall.

Once I know the bedding area's interior — and learn where the bucks prefer to bed — I'll try to find a few stand sites. I return to the edge of the bedding area and slowly walk around its perimeter. Whenever possible, I scout this entire edge. While I study every active runway I find, I'm most interested in those with large rubs.

After finishing this assessment, I review everything I've noticed. I first weed out the rub lines that were apparently made by small bucks. I also eliminate big-buck rub lines that show minimal rub activity. This leaves me with a handful of rub lines to scout for stand sites. These rub lines generate the most travel by big bucks, which means my stand sites will have the most potential for success.

How close to the bedding area should you place your stands? I like to set up close enough to feel confident I will see some daylight buck activity. However, I also try to stay far enough away from bedding areas to enter and leave my stands without alerting the bucks. Those guidelines are easily accomplished when bedding areas cover many acres. It's a different story when a bedding area is two acres or smaller. That's why it's important to thoroughly scout during the post-season to know exactly where bucks

You'll be forced to sacrifice valuable hunting time if you don't select stand sites beforehand for various wind directions. I implore you to take care of this critical task in the post-season.

usually bed. Obviously, it's difficult to know how close to set up to bedding areas if you don't know the preferred bedding sites.

Give Yourself Some Options

You'll be forced to sacrifice valuable hunting time if you don't select stand sites beforehand for various wind directions. I implore you to take care of this critical task in the post-season. I often prepare stand sites on both sides of rub lines that take a north/south route. This ensures I'll be able to hunt the spot with easterly or westerly winds. To state the obvious, I do the same thing with east/west rub lines to ensure I can hunt northerly or southerly winds. It really is that simple!

When I start spring rub-line scouting, I basically mirror my post-season forays. In fact, you should use this same approach, whether you're finding and following rub lines or invading bedding areas and selecting stand sites.

You'll hurt your spring-time missions if you try to combine rub-line scouting with shed-antler hunting. I think this is a big reason so many hunters have trouble deciphering rub lines. If you're in the woods to hunt sheds, you must only look for sheds. And if you're in the woods to hunt rub lines, you must only scout for rub lines! Trying to do both will hurt your efforts on both fronts. You'll struggle to decipher a big buck's rub lines if your attention is continually sidetracked.

Finding Good Stands During the Season

It's imperative to have an effective game plan for finding productive stands during the open season. Even though post-season rub-line scouting is important, there are no absolutes in deer hunting. Big bucks don't always use the same rub lines each year. Be prepared to move if they literally take a different avenue.

Also, if you get permission to hunt new tracts of land after the season opens, you must be ready to effectively scout those lands. Furthermore, there's the unpleasant reality of increases in hunting pressure. If the pressure becomes intense, big bucks often suddenly abandon their normal routes and establish new ones. Unless you're skilled at finding and deciphering rub

Many deer hunters make a critical mistake when they hit the woods in spring. They think they can combine a shed-hunting foray with rub-line scouting. Don't try it. When unraveling rub lines, you must give the effort your full attention. If you want to hunt for sheds, make that the sole purpose of your trip.

Every extra minute you spend in the woods scouting during the open season increases the chances that deer will catch on to your game plan. Speed-scouting, in which you hit the woods, look around, and get back out within one hour is your best bet for hunting unpressured deer.

lines, you could be out of the game all season.

In-season scouting for killer stands differs from off-season scouting in two important respects. Most obviously, unless it's your only option, avoid walking through suspected bedding areas during the season. Also, instead of spending many hours scouting prospective areas, you must drastically cut the time you spend in the woods. You should head into the woods, spend a little time scouting and selecting stand sites, and then quickly get out. Ideally, a speed-scouting/stand-selection trip should last no more than an hour.

If you want mature bucks to walk by within range of your stand, they can't feel they're being hunted. It's virtually impossible to keep them feeling unpressured if you spend many hours each day scouting their rub lines.

Speed-scouting is perfectly suited to finding good rub-line stand sites, but it might bother some of you. However, remember that your scouting entails finding the most visible and telling sign made by bucks. Even in early fall, fresh rubs are easier to spot than any other type of buck sign. And rubs become even more visible as

If your first choice in a stand site proves to be slightly off, don't despair. Watch, listen and pinpoint a better spot closer to the action. You should expect to make occasional minor adjustments in stand placement. Besides, watching from a stand is a hunter's least intrusive way to "scout" an area.

*Every extra minute you spend in the woods
during the open season increases the likelihood
the deer you're hunting will catch on to your gig.*

fall progresses. Not only do the woods thin out more each day to increase visibility, but the number of rubs also continues to grow.

Unfortunately, those same things often cause hunters to increase their scouting time as the pre-rut unfolds. Cooler temperatures also prompt hunters to get itchy feet. No matter the temptation, remember that every extra minute you spend in the woods increases the likelihood the deer you're hunting will catch on to your gig.

Pinpointing the Perfect Spot

My speed-scouting forays almost always start near feeding areas. However, unlike the off-season, I won't thoroughly scout each active big-buck rub line I find. Instead, I dedicate all my scouting to one or two rub lines. Unless I already know the area, I carry a topo map and an aerial photo while speed-scouting. After getting a "line" on where the rubs are heading, I study the map and photo and use some common sense to follow a rub line just far enough to find productive stand sites.

Realize, too, that because you can only spend a short time scouting, your stands will sometimes be slightly out of position. This happens to everyone, no matter their depth of experience. To remedy the situation, pay close attention to everything you see and hear during prime times for deer movement. If you're fortunate, you'll see and/or hear something to help you decide where to move your stand to make your hunt more productive.

While I would much rather have actual sightings of big bucks, I've used the sounds of sparring, rubbing or grunting to pinpoint killer stand sites. By the way, gathering such valuable information from your stand is the least intrusive way to scout your area.

Be Aggressive, But Be Careful!

While I encourage you to aggressively follow up on sounds, sightings and fresh sign, always remember that you're invading routes where bucks feel the most safe and secure. Never forget that rub lines are laid out along the bucks' most preferred travel routes. Don't let your aggressiveness override your common sense. Killer rub-line stands can only maintain their reputation if bucks are totally unaware of the hunters who use them.

Greg's Practical Points ━━━━━━━

➤ *Not all rub lines are created equal. Forests and deer woods hold far more unproductive than productive rub-line stand sites.*

➤ *Fresh rubs and reworked rubs found in the post-season can tell you exactly which rub lines bucks prefer to use.*

➤ *Bucks like certain travel routes for a reason, and barring a dramatic change in the habitat or landscape, several generations of bucks will sometimes use preferred routes indefinitely.*

➤ *Choosing killer stands means finding sites with the most potential. In many cases you won't find them unless you first eliminate all other possible sites.*

➤ *By walking around in bedding areas in the off-season, you can learn how a buck prefers to enter and leave daytime hideouts. This information is invaluable for locating the most productive rub-line stands.*

➤ *Prepare stands on both sides of rub lines. This ensures you can usually hunt the spot no matter the wind's direction.*

➤ *You'll hurt your spring-time missions if you try to combine rub-line scouting with shed-antler hunting. If you're in the woods to hunt sheds, you must only look for sheds!*

➤ *If you must scout during the season, make it snappy. Ideally, a speed-scouting/stand-selection trip should last no more than an hour.*

➤ *Killer rub-line stands can only maintain their reputation if bucks are totally unaware of the hunters who use them.*

White-tailed bucks relate to their rub lines in the early season, but finding and scouting rub lines at this time can be tough because of dense cover. Don't use lush cover as an excuse for not getting back into the woods to catch bucks that are moving at the edge of daylight.

Chapter 8

HOW EARLY CAN YOU HUNT RUB LINES?

O ne question people often ask is how early in fall bucks establish rub lines. If you don't know when bucks establish rub lines, you also don't know how soon you can hunt rub lines.

I admit being somewhat puzzled by this information gap. In addition to the information I've provided in magazines, books and seminars the past 10 years, many other writers and educators have jumped on the rub-line bandwagon. But while deer hunters have been deluged with rub-line information, I've found that some communicators don't pass along vital aspects of rub-line behavior.

The critical aspect that's commonly missed is early-season rub-line behavior. That might be because some so-called experts have little or no knowledge on this time period.

To be fair, most hunters haven't done much to help themselves, either. Too many of them prefer to wait in ambush along the edges of feeding

This rub is part of a rub line I hunted during a recent early season. Over the first three weeks of bow season I saw five different bucks along this rub line. Unfortunately, they all stayed outside my effective range.

areas in the early season. That is pretty much a no-brainer tactic. I won't argue it isn't occasionally effective on mature whitetails. Unfortunately, those occasional successes encourage hunters to keep using the tactic. They then refuse to explore the possibility of more productive early-season strategies. It's impossible to know what's going on inside the woods if you seldom venture more than a few yards from open feeding areas.

Of course, some hunters will say thick foliage and underbrush make it virtually impossible to scout effectively. Not true! Yes, early-season scouting can be difficult, but it's certainly not impossible.

Early Rub Lines Do Exist

Allow me to explain. White-tailed bucks are purposeful in their wanderings. Keep that in mind when scouting rub lines. Why? Even though it might not look like it, each rub line has a definite beginning and ending, and most endings are near food sources and bedding areas. Most bucks travel between bedding and feeding areas from the time they shed their velvet until the time they start breeding. These predictable

While it's possible to catch big bucks near feeding areas during the early season, your chances for action are greater if you set up along active rub lines leading to feeding areas. You don't always have to go that far back in. Sometimes 100 yards will get the job done.

patterns are never more evident than during the early season. In my region, this means mid- to late September.

My son, Jake, and I used this time of predictable buck behavior to our benefit recently. We were pre-season scouting in the second week of September at one of our favorite big-woods areas when we found two distinct, active rub lines.

Obviously, this is not when most hunters are looking for rub lines. However, as is often the case in early fall, we didn't find many large rubs. But we did find many shredded clumps of red osier dogwood and tag alder brush. We also discovered many saplings that had been rubbed clean and snapped off. Dozens of earlier, similar experiences taught me this type of rubbing activity usually indicates at least one better-than-average buck.

Reasons for Early Rub Sign

It would be a gross understatement to say this early rub sign was encouraging. But even though it was early autumn (actually, late

Water sources can play a significant role in where big bucks establish their early-season rub lines. This is especially true in years when temperatures are unusually hot and rainfall is in short supply.

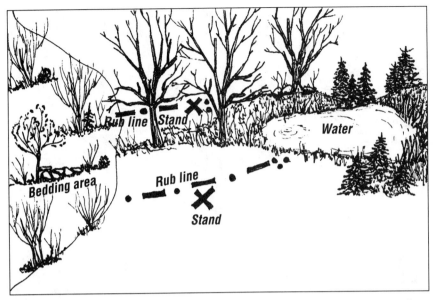

Rub lines that link bedding areas with water sources often attract tremendous amounts of buck travel during the early season. Try placing your stands near the water. Trust me, bucks hit water holes throughout autumn more often than some "experts" would have you believe.

summer!) I wasn't that surprised for two reasons. First, a lush alfalfa field was just a quarter-mile from where Jake and I were scouting. And second, although we didn't find it until later, a small, spring-fed water hole was near our stands.

As is usually the case wherever agricultural crops bump up to big woods, the alfalfa was attracting many deer. However, the water hole was the real draw in those early season hunts. Warm daytime temperatures, coupled with drought-like conditions, had made water a top priority for area whitetails. As Jake and I discovered, deer flocked to the little water hole in the mornings and evenings.

Because it was my intent from the beginning to get Jake within bow range of a buck, I placed his stand along what looked like the most active of two rub lines we found. During the season's first month, he saw dozens of deer from his stand, including several monsters. But only a long-horned spike walked past his stand within bow range. At the time, Jake considered a spike to be a target animal, but his arrow whizzed a hair's width over the buck's back.

The rub line I was hunting hadn't looked as promising as Jake's when we set up. Even so, I had some excitement. On two occasions a bachelor

My son, Jake, looks at an early-season rub. Heat, thick foliage and biting insects can make scouting difficult at this time of year, but as we've discovered, the rewards usually justify the effort.

group of four bucks, including two shooters, paraded by just past my effective bow range. And on a brisk, windy morning in late September, I got the surprise of my life. About 30 minutes after daylight I noticed a flicker of movement to my left. I turned my head to see a huge 10-point buck walk out of some thick tag alders 50 yards away. The 150-class whitetail continued easing toward me along his rub line until he was 15 yards away. Just as he was about to step into the clear, he sensed things weren't right.

It's possible to realize early-season success with minimal scouting. The trick is to find areas that aren't pressured too heavily, and then locate rub lines from the previous year. This could indicate a preferred travel route.

Rather than panicking and bounding off, the buck slowly turned and walked back the way he'd come. That was the last I saw of him. Interestingly, this rub line became a bit less active after that day. Even though I had taken every precaution to keep it from happening, the big buck had apparently detected me.

Food and Water are Early-Season Keys

Several things can be learned from that early-season experience. First, it proved bucks of all sizes relate to rubs and rub lines during the early season. Second, even mature bucks can sometimes be caught moving along rub lines in daylight during the early season. And last, the location of preferred foods and water play a huge role in where bucks make rub lines.

While the location of preferred foods is important, it's the water that demands the closest look. I've long believed in the important role that water plays in the daily lives of whitetails in the early season. But even

Your chances for success later in the season often hinge on the type of behavior you display during the early season. Bucks are tuned into their areas in early fall, and will quickly change their movement patterns if they detect regular human activity. Chances are, these changes will be so subtle you'll have few clues that they've altered their activities.

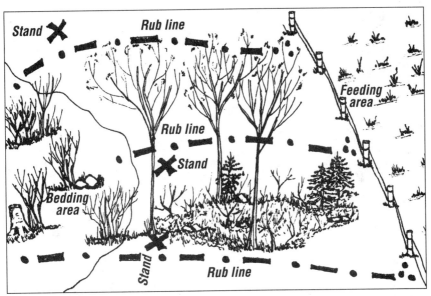

Big bucks sometimes can be caught in or at the edge of feeding areas during the early season. However, don't let a little success with this tactic fool you. Catching bucks in these openings during daylight is far more the exception than the rule. You'll see more consistent results by hunting back in the woods.

though I've always preached its importance, many bow-hunters still concentrate all their early-season efforts on feeding areas.

While that is occasionally effective and possibly the only option available, you'll almost always have better early-season success by hunting along rub lines that link bedding areas to water sources. This is especially true during unusually hot or dry weather.

Scouting for Early Rub Lines

Although whitetails normally eat a variety of foods at this time of year, they almost always prefer one over all else. In fact, this behavior holds true much of the season, but it's especially important to remember in early fall. Here's why. Before you can expect to locate, follow and set up along early-season rub lines, you must know the exact location of preferred deer foods. The only way you'll find out is to do some scouting and homework in your hunting area.

Like many novice hunters, I used to concentrate my early-season efforts on the outside perimeters of feeding areas. But this tactic is seldom productive when hunting pressure is even slightly intense. You're much better off setting up along travel routes some distance back from

It's possible to hunt bucks in velvet along rub lines from previous years. This fact can benefit those who live or hunt in areas where the archery season opens before bucks shed their velvet.

feeding areas. Still, it's much easier to talk about this strategy than it is to put it into practice.

I never had much trouble finding and figuring out rub lines during the middle and latter stages of the pre-rut. But I admit those tasks are more difficult during the early season when thick foliage and leafy underbrush reduce visibility. Also, other than an initial flurry of rubbing after velvet shedding, bucks usually aren't "rub active" in early fall.

I stumbled onto a strategy that has proven effective for dealing with those negatives. Instead of trying to follow early rub-lines in their entirety, I follow them 100 yards or so from feeding/watering areas before looking for suitable stand sites. Remember, this is a time when bucks normally are active and highly predictable in their travels.

Unless hunting pressure is heavy, I can get away with setting up relatively close to feeding/watering areas. This is far more effective than waiting along the edge of feeding areas.

So, unless hunting pressure is heavy, I can get away with setting up relatively close to feeding/watering areas. This is far more effective than waiting along the edge of feeding areas. What's more, it usually entails a minimum of scouting, which reduces the chance you'll "booger" up a potentially productive situation.

Another Early Rub-Line Strategy

I'll occasionally take a chance during the early season and set up along a rub line without thoroughly scouting the area. I only do this when I cannot do any pre-season or in-season scouting.

This happens at times because I like to hunt totally new areas when I need a break from my favorite spots. Unfortunately, I don't always have my back-up spots prepared. That's when I take a chance and set up along a "traditional" rub line. These are rub lines that are used year after year, so I don't get discouraged if I don't see fresh rubs along the rub line near my stand. I figure it's possible several bucks are using the rub line fairly regularly, but they just aren't especially rub-active yet. It could also be that my setups are in a gap between some rubs

A certain aspect of buck behavior is of special interest for early-season rub-line hunters, and I think many of you are aware of it: the tendency for bucks to still be in bachelor groups. Not only are the bucks bedding and feeding together, they're also traveling together. In many cases, all members of a bachelor group will use the same rub lines. If you happen to set up on one of these "hot" rub lines, it's possible every buck in the area could parade past you. Just remember that while bachelor groups can create wonderful opportunities, they can also create major problems. The more eyes, ears and noses near you, the greater the chance you'll be detected.

Another Reason to Tread Lightly

No matter where you hunt the early season, however, realize that some mature bucks refuse to move much in daylight at this time of year. Several big deer I've hunted over the years were in that category.

While scouting "foreign" lands, remember that bucks often use the same rub lines year after year. Immediately start looking for rubs and rub lines from previous years.

However, almost all of them became active in daylight late in the pre-rut, which made them susceptible to ambush from strategically placed stands. I've capitalized on such situations several times by taking every precaution to keep from being discovered.

Therein lies a critical point regarding rub lines that must always be stressed. Your chances anytime in autumn often hinge on your behavior during the early season. At no other time of year are whitetails so in tune with their surroundings. Big bucks miss little that goes on in their core areas. The slightest human odor or close call with a bow-hunter can make mature deer instantly alter their normal routines. Granted, those changes often can barely be noticed, yet they usually allow a buck to evade us, possibly for the remainder of the season.

No Fresh Rubs? No Problem!

I regularly bow-hunt several states and two Canadian provinces where archery seasons open while bucks are still in velvet. With no fresh rubs or rub lines to guide me, I at first felt lost while scouting these "foreign" lands. Then I remembered some rub-line basics, specifically that bucks often use the same rub lines year after year. I immediately started looking for rubs and rub lines from previous years. That approach quickly put me into bucks.

Hunting along early-season rub lines will always be a tough deal, but I consider this strategy among the most effective for killing mature bucks. Any effort you put into locating and scouting early rub-lines is energy well spent. And if you do succeed in killing a deer, the rewards will be just that much sweeter.

Greg's Practical Points

➤ *The tendency for bucks to spend most of their travel time moving between bedding and feeding areas is never more obvious than in late summer and early fall.*

➤ *When finding early-season rub lines, chances are they link a buck's bedding area to a water source or feeding area.*

➤ *Bucks of all sizes relate to rubs and rub lines during the early season. Just because you see a spike using the rub line doesn't mean a much bigger buck won't use it later.*

➤ *Even mature bucks can sometimes be caught moving along rub lines in daylight during the early season.*

➤ *Because bucks are often still in their bachelor groups in the early season, it's not unheard of to have a parade of bucks move along a rub line at this time of year.*

➤ *Although whitetails eat a variety of foods, they almost always prefer one over all else at a particular time. Before you can expect to locate, follow and set up along early-season rub lines, you must know the exact location of preferred deer foods.*

➤ *Because some rub lines are used year after year, don't get discouraged if you don't see fresh rubs along the rub line near your stand. It's possible several bucks are using the rub line regularly, but they just aren't yet rub-active.*

➤ *Some mature bucks refuse to move much in daylight in the early season. But almost all of them became active in daylight late in the pre-rut, which makes them susceptible to ambush from strategically placed stands.*

Big bucks become much more "daylight-active" during the pre-rut. Hunters often benefit from the change because much of this activity occurs near the edges of feeding areas.

Chapter 9

HUNTING
THE PRE-RUT

We've now come to my favorite chapter in this book. I feel that way for several reasons, but one stands high above the rest. Without question, rub-line hunting for big bucks is most productive during the lengthy pre-rut period. This is partly because bucks become increasingly more rub-active with each day. In addition, the once-thick foliage and dense underbrush is starting to thin. The ever-growing number of rubs, coupled with vastly increasing visibility, makes finding and following rub lines much easier.

More than anything, though, the most exciting factor is that even the biggest bucks are becoming more active in daylight along their rub lines. Provided you're careful, daylight rub-line activity will keep increasing as the pre-rut rolls along, and much of this daylight activity occurs near the edges of feeding areas.

Before continuing, I want to make sure you know what I mean

Mature bucks seldom leave their bedding areas in daylight during the October lull. When they do walk around, they move at night and they seldom wander. They head directly to specific sites and move with their survival senses turned to the highest settings.

During the October lull, I take every precaution to keep deer I'm hunting from detecting my presence. I don't want to do anything to call attention to where I'm hunting. For that reason, I don't call or rattle during the October lull.

when I use the term "pre-rut." This period encompasses the time between velvet shedding and breeding. Because we've already covered the early season, this chapter will discuss the time between the first week of October and the start of the rut.

For simplicity's sake and to avoid getting bogged down in regional differences, I'll use Nov. 1 as the rut's kick-off. No matter what the actual dates are in your area each year, the information in this chapter should prove helpful.

Dealing with the October Lull

While the pre-rut is my favorite time to hunt rub-line bucks, it includes a time that's extremely frustrating. This time frame, which is sandwiched between the early season and the middle of the pre-rut, is commonly called the October lull. In my home state, Wisconsin, this lull usually occurs about Oct. 7 to 20.

What is the October lull? I believe this is a time when bucks, especially mature animals, drastically reduce their travel while tremendously increasing their food intake. Unfortunately, this increased

I know of many mature bucks that were ambushed near feeding areas during the middle of the pre-rut. While big white-tailed bucks might occasionally relax their nighttime-only travel patterns at this time, they haven't lowered their guard.

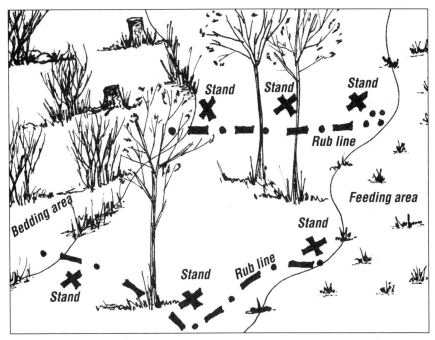

The location of your tree stand should be dictated by which stage of the pre-rut you're hunting. During the early days of the pre-rut — the October lull — you should place your rub-line stands almost within sight of a buck's bedding areas. In the middle of the pre-rut, hunt rub-line stands near field edges late in the day and near bedding areas in the morning. Toward the end of the pre-rut, place your stands almost anywhere along active rub lines.

feeding activity does not increase daytime movements.

I believe bucks do almost all of their traveling at night during the lull. A big buck typically just walks a rub line from his bedding area directly to a nearby food source. Although he might then travel to other feeding areas during the night, he won't wander much. Nor will he do much scraping and rubbing. And he will almost always be tucked deeply into his bedding area before daylight.

Hunters commonly say: "The bucks have to be moving in daylight somewhere. They're just not moving along the rub lines I'm hunting." That seldom happens during the October lull, but some hunters can't accept the fact that bigger bucks might not move at all during daylight. Instead of attributing deer-free hunts to natural occurrences, hunters convince themselves they're just in the wrong place. Therefore, they get into an all-out walking/scouting frenzy. Their intentions are well-meaning, but the results can be disastrous. They

It's OK to use rattling antlers and grunt calls during the middle of the pre-rut. Keep your calling sequences subtle and infrequent. Calling more than once per hour will do more to make bucks suspicious than it will to entice them.

As precious as hunting time might be, it's a good idea to spend less time in the woods during the October lull. This is especially true if you're trying to arrow a mature buck.

end up bumping deer that are already nervous and flighty, and the bucks become even more nocturnal. If spooked bad enough and often enough, big bucks might continue their nocturnal tendencies well into the middle of the pre-rut.

This is one time when drastically reducing your in-the-woods time might increase your chances of killing a mature buck. Certainly, no serious deer hunter likes to take a break, because all hunting time remains precious, even in states with lengthy archery seasons. But as precious as hunting time might be, it's still a good idea to spend less time in the woods during the October lull.

I usually hunt the lull by popping into an area, spending an hour or two on a rub-line stand early in the morning and late in the day, and then quietly leaving. Each of my hunts will be in a totally different area, and I never hunt the same stand two days in a row.

I also don't do anything to draw attention to my position. I don't blow on a grunt call or bang rattling antlers. Call me paranoid, but I believe big bucks are especially suspicious of such sounds during the lull. Besides cutting back on rubbing and scraping, bucks in the midst of the October lull aren't distracted by hot does and aggressive competing bucks. That allows them to focus all their attention on their surroundings. They hear every suspicious sound, they see every suspicious movement, and they most assuredly sniff every suspicious trace of human odor. Remember what I constantly say about being careful when scouting and hunting big-buck rub lines? Extreme care is never more important than during the October lull!

The Middle Pre-Rut

The middle of the pre-rut falls between the October lull and the late pre-rut. The number of rubs and scrapes increases noticeably, as does daylight buck activity. Even so, hunters will have their best chance of seeing rub-line buck activity by hunting stands near bedding areas.

This doesn't mean big bucks never show up near feeding areas during the middle of the pre-rut. I've seen my share of such activity

Buck activity on rub lines increases sharply late in the pre-rut. It doesn't matter where you place your stands along active rub lines. Once bucks become active, they could show up anywhere along their travel routes.

How do you decide which rub line to hunt? Wind conditions will eliminate some possibilities. Like it or not, though, choosing the right rub line often means trusting your instincts.

and ambushed bucks near feeding areas during this time, but each big-buck encounter occurred in the early evening. That's why you're best served to place your morning rub-line stands near bedding areas.

As with the early season, finding productive rub-line stand sites for the middle pre rut can be tough. Even though there is more buck sign to help you, there will be times when it's spread equally over several runways. How do you decide which rub line to hunt? Of course, wind conditions will always eliminate some possibilities. Like it or not, though, choosing the right rub line often means trusting your instincts. This approach will result in some "close-but-no-cigar" situations. You'll see some buck activity, but not always within range.

That can be frustrating, but there are some guidelines to follow. You must watch everything the buck does and note exactly where he walks. Remember this information and then return during a safer scouting time. Closely check where you saw the buck walk to see if you can find a regular route. If you even suspect you've found his trail, move your stand and hunt the spot immediately.

Calling During the Middle Pre-Rut

Calling can be effective during the middle pre-rut, but over-calling can ruin what would have been a productive rub-line site. Remember, the October lull has just ended. The bucks are a bit more curious, but they're still suspicious. Might they respond to calling? Your guess is as good as mine. Some bucks I've called to at this time turned and ran. Others stood and stared in my direction, and some just ignored me. A few responded exactly the way I wanted. You never know.

When calling at this time I avoid the deep-pitched "bull-of-the-woods" grunt calls. I prefer to imitate the grunt of an immature buck, and blow the call softly. Use a similar subtle approach to rattling. Bring the antlers together gently and softly "tickle" the tines for 15 to 30 seconds. This type of rattling more closely resembles sparring matches that occur this time of year.

Use your grunt calls and rattling antlers sparingly. Big bucks aren't

In cases where rubs appear to be spread equally over several travel routes, I set up along rub lines that also contain many scrapes. Sometimes you must accept the fact you won't know for certain that you've found a buck's most active rub line. A strong combination of rub and scrape activity tends to tip the scales in my decision-making process.

Hunting the late pre-rut fits my preference for singling out several big bucks to hunt during the season. Because breeding rituals haven't begun, I know these bucks are still in their core areas.

too vocal at this time, nor are they having many head-to-head encounters. I suggest no more than one calling sequence per hour. I believe calling more often than that only makes big bucks more suspicious, not more interested. In fact, I seldom do any calling during my middle pre-rut hunts. I put my efforts into precise stand placement and my faith into natural rub-line movements.

The Late Pre-Rut

While bucks relate to their rub lines the entire time they carry hard antlers, this relationship is never stronger than during the late pre-rut. At no other time are bucks reworking and making rubs so frequently. Increased rub activity and the buck's strong attachment to preferred rub lines makes it easier to figure out big-buck movements.

Another good thing about hunting the late pre-rut is that it fits my preference for singling out several big bucks to hunt throughout the season. Because breeding rituals haven't begun, I know these bucks are still in their core areas. I also know their tendencies can be patterned. You seldom have either of those luxuries once the rut kicks in.

For much of the pre-rut, rub-line stands near bedding areas will produce the most consistent big-buck activity. That can change dramatically in latter stages of the pre-rut. It's now possible to catch big bucks skulking along their rub lines near the edge of feeding areas in the morning and evening.

Even with increased daylight buck movements, you must continue to speed-scout to find the hottest rub lines in your area. Don't worry about finding the most productive spots along a rub line. At this time, you can set up near the rub line's ends or midsections, and it really doesn't matter which spot you choose. Because bucks are moving during daylight, any part of a rub line can be productive.

If every rub line you find in the late pre-rut looks good, how do you decide which ones are used the most? Actually, I'm not convinced I've always found a buck's most active rub lines. In cases where rub

One of the best times for calling in mature bucks is the final week of the pre-rut, and tree stands along active rub lines are by far the most productive places to call from. I think this is because bucks establish rub lines along routes where they feel the safest, and a buck is more likely to approach an unseen buck if he feels the route is secure.

numbers seem equally distributed on several rub lines, I concentrate on rub lines where I find the most rubs and scrapes.

Bucks often remain in their bachelor groups into the late pre-rut. During late October a few years ago, I had barely settled into my stand when a forkhorn walked into view. He wasn't a shooter, but I lifted my bow from its hanger. That proved wise, because a pig-like grunt suddenly sounded in thick brush behind the little buck. I looked that way and saw a slightly larger buck walk out. The 6-pointer stared at the forkhorn for several seconds, and then both deer walked by within easy bow range.

They had just walked out of sight when I heard another loud grunt. A third buck was soon strolling toward me. This basket-racked buck was trailing the first two bucks. Thinking I had seen my share of buck action for the day, I was startled when a fourth buck walked out, this one considerably larger than the rest. The heavy-beamed 8-pointer was going to walk within 10 yards of my stand. I knew I would shoot

Some hunters become increasingly careless as bucks become more visible. Not only do they overhunt favorite stands, but they take more chances with the wind. Those are big mistakes.

this buck if it gave me a chance.

Just as I started to draw, I heard another buck grunting! It was obvious from the 8-pointer's reaction that this fifth buck was the boss. The 10-pointer that soon appeared boasted substantially larger antlers and a much thicker neck. And this big deer looked like it would waltz down the same runway the smaller bucks had taken! That 10-yard shot was one of the easiest I've ever had at a trophy whitetail.

Before moving on, let me add one more piece of advice. I've noticed some hunters become increasingly careless as bucks become more visible. Not only do they overhunt favorite stands, but they take more chances with the wind. Both are costly mistakes. Regardless of how it might appear, big bucks haven't lowered their guard. They're just as alert and predator-conscious as ever.

Calling Bucks During the Late Pre-Rut

One of the best times for calling in mature bucks is the final week of the pre-rut, and tree stands along active rub lines are by far the most productive places to call from. I think this is because bucks establish rub lines along routes where they feel the safest, and a buck is more likely to approach an unseen buck if he feels the route is secure.

Unfortunately, this is where many hunters fail in their efforts to kill large bucks. They seem to think they can walk into the woods anywhere, bang antlers together, toot on a grunt call, and wait for a big buck to run in. That ain't gonna happen! To generate positive responses, you must call from sites that big bucks can approach while feeling safe.

I once rattled in and arrowed a dandy big-woods 10-pointer. Several factors contributed to my success. During the post-season, I had scouted the buck's home range and unraveled a couple of his rub lines. I had also pinpointed where he was bedding, and had actually stood in one of his beds.

I had also picked a couple of possible stand sites. I hunted from one

Suddenly, he was there. The 10-pointer thrashed a clump of tag alders before moving into bow range. Ironically, he was standing on one of his rub lines when my arrow struck.

of those sites early in the season, but then stayed away until the final week of the pre-rut. Thirty minutes after settling onto my stand, I made a loud, aggressive rattling sequence. I had barely hung up the antlers when I heard a deer approaching from a bedding area I had found in the post-season. It seemed to take forever for the deer to step clear of the thick spruce swamp in front of me. Then he was suddenly there. The 10-pointer thrashed a clump of tag alders before moving into bow range. Ironically, he was standing on one of his rub lines when my arrow struck.

During the late pre-rut, my calling is much more intense and louder than during the middle pre-rut. I also might call a bit more frequently, and I begin each sequence with a loud and sometimes lengthy mock-rubbing session.

I think mock rubbing is the most important aspect of my late pre-rut calling sequences. After all, I'm set up in a spot where a big buck has already been rubbing. Because bucks use their rubs as signposts, mock rubbing tells bucks within earshot that another buck has trespassed onto its turf. More importantly, the trespasser has an aggressive attitude, and a resident buck is especially touchy about such things late in the pre-rut.

What is Patterning?

I've talked a lot in this chapter about being able to "pattern" big bucks. I hope I haven't misled you. While we might be able to figure out where big bucks will walk, there's no foolproof system for figuring out when those bucks will appear. Patience and persistence will always be a deer hunter's strongest allies, and they're best invested along active rub lines in the late pre-rut.

Greg's Practical Points

➤ *Rub-line hunting for big bucks is most productive during the pre-rut, partly because bucks become increasingly more rub-active and daylight-active each day.*

➤ *Another advantage hunters have in the pre-rut is that leaves begin to fall, allowing for greater visibility and easier scouting.*

➤ *The October lull is a time when bucks, especially mature animals, drastically reduce their travel while tremendously increasing their food intake. Unfortunately, they seldom move during the day at this time.*

➤ *During the middle of the pre-rut, the number of rubs and scrapes increases noticeably, as does daylight buck activity. Still, your best chance of seeing rub-line buck activity is by hunting stands near bedding areas.*

➤ *When calling during the middle pre-rut, avoid deep-pitched grunt calls. I imitate the grunt of an immature buck, and blow the call softly.*

➤ *Bucks rework and make new rubs frequently late in the pre-rut. Increased rub activity and the buck's attachment to a rub line makes it easier to figure out big-buck movements.*

➤ *For much of the pre-rut, rub-line stands near bedding areas will produce the most consistent big-buck activity. That can change dramatically late in the pre-rut.*

➤ *In cases where rub numbers seem equally distributed on several rub lines, I concentrate on rub lines where I find the most rubs and scrapes.*

I've had hundreds of memorable rub-line experiences over the years. While I appreciate and cherish each of them, some are more special than others. This chapter tells the story about the best textbook example I've ever seen of a rub line and how it led me to a big buck.

Chapter 10

A CLASSIC PRE-RUT RUB-LINE HUNT

I've had so many big buck experiences along rub lines during the pre-rut that I can't remember them all. I'm sure I forgot some simply because of the many years that have slipped by since the day they occurred. I've forgotten others because I just got glimpses of big bucks. Unfortunately, I've probably forgotten a few others because I'm at that age when I often have trouble remembering what I meant to do next.

Even so, many rub-line memories remain almost as vivid as the day the incident occurred, and some are more special than the others. One of those special memories happened recently during a classic rub-line bow-hunt near my home in Wisconsin.

Some Valuable Post-Season Discoveries
This story begins in February. My son, Jake, and I were post-season

I had arrowed this beautiful 10-pointer while hunting a favorite spot in Wisconsin. Unfortunately, the next winter, loggers dumped a pile of discarded timber atop the runway where my killer stand had been situated.

The big buck we were tracking led us into the heart of his core area. There was buck sign everywhere! Even though the snow was only a day old, deer had already beaten an obvious trail through it.

scouting in an area where I had bow-killed a beautiful 10-point buck the previous fall. Fresh snow covered the ground, which made scouting conditions ideal. When we drove in, we discovered loggers had just select-cut some large oaks and maples. This wasn't necessarily bad news, but a large pile of discarded timber blocked a the runway where I had arrowed the 10-pointer.

"There's no sense wasting our time here," I told Jake. "Let's check out the other end of the property."

That proved to be a wise decision. Jake and I were crossing a picked cornfield when we saw fresh deer tracks in the snow ahead. Before we got close I could tell the tracks were made by a big deer. When we reached the hoofprints, I realized they were as large as any I had ever seen.

"Well, it looks like one big buck survived gun season last fall," I said. "Hopefully, he'll stick around until bow season."

Above, my daughter, Jessie, and I went back to the area in October for a follow-up scouting job. It didn't take long to figure out what the big buck was doing. The buck left a rub line so obvious that Jessie could almost walk from rub to rub as she unraveled it with me.

Partly out of curiosity and partly because the tracks were going our way, we followed them. They led to the top of a wooded bluff before turning in another direction. At that point, we left the buck's trail and started scouting for sign from the previous fall. Within minutes we realized the buck had led us into the heart of his core area. Buck sign was everywhere. We found big rubs, small rubs and medium-sized rubs. We also found a well-used runway along the upper rim of a huge bowl. Though the snow was only one day old, the runway was hammered with deer tracks, including a huge set of hoofprints.

Jake and I followed the runway to the top of a narrow hog's-back ridge, where we made an interesting discovery. Nearly 30 years earlier I had helped the landowner build a four-strand barbwire fence through this section of bluff. The fence was now on the ground where it crossed the ridge. No wonder every deer passing through the area used this runway. They were taking advantage of this gap in the fence.

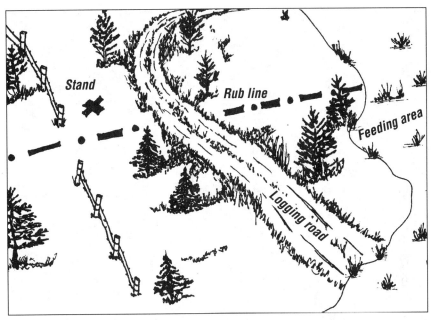

The big buck in this chapter had marked a classic rub line through the woods. The rub line extended from the edge of open crop land all the way to the buck's bedding area. My stand was near a spot on a ridge where the rub line led through a downed, in-woods fence line. That put me within 75 yards of the buck's bedding area.

Jake and I spent another couple of hours that day scouting the buck's core area. By the time we left, I was confident we had figured out where he was bedding. I was also confident that if the buck stuck around until next fall, one of us had a good chance of having him walk by within bow range.

The Autumn Return

The next time I entered the buck's home range was Oct. 12. My son was busy with football practice, so I asked my 10 year-old daughter, Jessie, if she wanted to do some scouting. She jumped at the chance. As we were driving, I explained to Jessie some things about the October lull. I stressed that we must be careful where we walked and that we could not raise our voices. She seemed comfortable with my rules.

We had been in the woods a few minutes when Jessie found the first rub. The buck had roughed up a maple about 3 inches thick — better than average for the area. Judging by the sapling's shine, it was

Unseasonably warm temperatures had kept the woods from "thinning out" even a little that fall. Maybe conditions would improve during the two weeks I would be away on other commitments.

We had gone only a short distance before Jessie suddenly stopped, pointed and whispered excitedly, "There's another rub, Dad, and it's bigger than the other ones!"

---

evident the buck had put a lot of effort into the rub. Still, I wasn't overly excited. My mood changed considerably when Jessie found two more similar rubs 50 yards from the first one.

"Let's keep following this runway to see if we can find some more rubs," I said. "Maybe we can figure out where this ol' buck is going."

Excited at the prospect of doing some honest-to-goodness scouting, Jessie led the way. We had gone only a short distance before she suddenly stopped, pointed and whispered excitedly, "There's another rub, Dad, and it's bigger than the other ones!" I eased up beside her and saw she wasn't exaggerating. It was much bigger than the others.

Now I was intense. We walked another 75 yards and found two more rubs. We now stood where Jake and I had abandoned the buck's trail the previous winter. From where we stood, we could see how the bluff descended gradually to agricultural ground below. I studied the surroundings while thinking about the rubs.

The Destination Becomes Obvious

"I know what this buck is doing, Jessie," I blurted out. Pointing to the fields far below, I said: "He's feeding in those fields down there at night. Then he uses this runway to go back to his bedding area in the morning. I've got a feeling I know exactly where he's bedding."

We found several more rubs before the runway led us onto an old logging road. Our search then became tougher. It was obvious the rub line didn't continue straight across the logging road.

"It looks like he's walking right down this old road," I said. "He'll turn onto another runway eventually. I just hope we find some more rubs to help us figure out which runway he's using."

We went about 25 yards when Jessie spotted another large rub on the opposite side of the logging trail. As we eased up to it, I quietly said we had to be much more cautious.

"We're only about 100 yards from where Jake and I found that bedding area last winter," I said. "Let's keep going and see if this rub line leads us to that fence-crossing I told you about."

Here I am with the results of my classic rub-line hunt. The big 9-pointer had a rough gross antler score in the 140s and a field-dressed weight of 214 pounds.

The winds had been southerly, but were supposed to switch to the northwest. I knew such changes often jump-start deer activity. Perhaps I would catch the big buck moving.

Jessie nodded and led the way. Less than 20 yards later, we found a fresh scrape, and 25 yards beyond was another rub. I could now see the fence-crossing. I could also see a fresh rub on a forearm-sized birch tree next to the fence-crossing. I had seen enough.

Bending down, I whispered that our scouting excursion was finished. "We're getting real close to where I believe the buck is bedding," I said. "The deer are very touchy at this time of year, so we'd better not go any farther. I'm going to come back alone in a few days and get some stands prepared along this rub line. Maybe I can get a shot at the buck that's making all these rubs."

Business commitments prevented me from hunting the rub line the week after we discovered it. I then spent the next week chasing whitetails in northern Missouri with my good friend David Forbes. Looking back, I think those "previous engagements" were a good thing. For one thing, the deer were entrenched in the October lull the week after Jessie found the rub line. And the next week brought record-high daytime temperatures to our region. Neither situation is conducive to rub-line hunting.

The Hunt

I returned from my Missouri hunt Oct. 25. The next morning, I hunted from a stand along the rub line. The day started out cool, but the temperature rose fast when the sun peeked over the horizon. I saw no deer that morning, and when I hunted the rub line from a different stand that afternoon, I saw no deer again. However, I heard one walk by just as I was preparing to climb down. The deer was just over the ridge, so I couldn't see it.

I stayed away from the rub line for a day, and when hearing the weather forecast, I made plans to return to the area the morning of Oct. 28. The winds had been southerly in previous weeks, but were supposed to switch to the northwest. I knew such changes often jump-start deer activity. Perhaps I would catch the big buck moving.

If he continued on his course, he would pass at 30 yards in thick brush. That wouldn't provide a good shot. Then the trophy whitetail surprised me. He turned and walked right at me.

The Buck Appears

At dawn the next morning I was in a slight panic after leaving home 15 minutes later than I should have. The only positive thing about arriving late was that I could walk to my stand without using a flashlight. After reaching my tree, climbing 15 feet to the portable stand, and organizing all my gear, I sat back and tried to relax. Ten minutes later I was still scolding myself for the late start.

Then I heard the first deer approaching. I stood slowly, grabbed my bow and peered toward the sounds. Before long, four antlerless deer walked into sight. The last deer in the group, a mature doe, kept stopping and looking back over her rump. Try as I might, I couldn't hear or see anything that indicated another deer was tagging along behind. Pressing tightly against the tree, I scarcely breathed as the does and fawns moved within 10 yards of my tree.

The foursome milled around in front of me for a few minutes, and then snapped their heads erect and stared at their back-trail. I looked where they were staring and heard a deer walking through leaves. Seconds later, a loud grunt erupted from just over the ridge. I had no doubt about the sex of the fifth deer! I shifted my feet to a better shooting position and waited for the buck to appear.

The wait wasn't long. The first thing I noticed was that he was a shooter. I also noticed he wasn't following his rub line. If he continued on his course, he would pass at 30 yards. Considering the thick brush between us, I wouldn't have a good shot. About the time I was ready to proclaim the experience a "close-but-no-cigar" deal, the trophy whitetail surprised me. He turned and walked right at me. While this brought him quickly into bow range, it also put him at an impossible shooting angle. All I could do was watch and pray he would turn and offer a better shot.

Moving In

The big deer continued to close the distance while remaining head-on. At one point the buck stopped to sniff and lick a rub Jessie and I

I've been hunting big bucks along their rub-lines for nearly 20 years. Not once in all that time have I seen a more classic example of a rub line than the one my daughter and I found in October 1998.

had found two weeks earlier. After completing this ritual, he took a couple of more steps toward me, which put him on the trail I had used to reach my stand. The buck instantly dropped his head and sniffed my tracks.

Fortunately, I had liberally sprayed my boots with doe urine before walking into the woods. The buck obviously liked the smell, because he turned and followed my trail. He was now broadside five yards from the base of my tree. I came to full draw, locked the top sight pin on his vitals and released the arrow. The hog-bodied whitetail crouched at the hit, spun to his right and bounded over a nearby ridge. I thought I heard him fall a few seconds later.

I remained on my stand until I was fully composed, and then climbed down and walked to where he had stood when I shot. I instantly found the start of an obvious blood trail. Confident the

Many hunters struggle with rub-line hunting, because they expect every rub line to be marked in classic fashion. But only a few mature bucks have obvious, easily exploitable rubbing tendencies.

razor-sharp broadhead had done its job, I immediately took up the trail. I had gone about 50 yards when I saw his still form on the ground. The long-tined 9-pointer gross-scored in the 140s, and his field-dressed weight was 214 pounds. By the way, he also had large hoofs, possibly the same ones that made the big tracks we had found the previous February.

Every aspect of my hunt for the 9-pointer was classic. Jake and I first learned of the big deer's presence while post-season scouting. That scouting trip also yielded valuable information regarding his core area, one of his preferred travel routes and, most importantly, the exact location of his bedding area. Jessie and I put the puzzle's remaining pieces together during our mid-October scouting trip.

Classic Rub Lines are Rare

Not once in my 20 years of rub-line hunting had I seen a more classic example of a rub line than the one Jessie and I found. No less than a dozen fresh rubs marked a quarter-mile stretch of the 9-pointer's morning travel route. The rub line also contained several active scrapes along its route. All this sign had made it relatively easy for my 10-year-old daughter to unravel his rub line.

Not until some time after that hunt did I give it some serious, objective thought. That's when it hit me. This is why many hunters struggle with rub-line hunting. They expect that every rub line they find will be marked in classic fashion. In reality, only a few mature bucks have such obvious, easily exploitable rubbing tendencies. In fact, not until that hunt in October 1998 had I seen such a classic example of a rub line. Yet I've still managed to rack up a fairly impressive string of rub-line successes over the years.

That just proves you don't always have to hunt along classic rub lines. It also proves rub behavior isn't as clear-cut as some hunters might believe.

Greg's Practical Points ———————

➤ *By following a set of big tracks in midwinter, you might learn the exact location of a big buck's bedding area.*

➤ *When finding a rub-line trail, try to figure out its purpose. Does it start in a feeding area that bucks leave early in the morning? Or does it start from a bedding area that bucks leave late in the day?*

➤ *When winds blow in hot air from the south for several days in mid- to late October, don't despair. When forecasters predict a wind shift more to the north, get ready to hunt. A wind switch to the northwest in late October often jump-starts buck activity.*

➤ *Don't panic if you get a late start. Don't be in such a rush to reach your stand that you forget to put masking scents on your boots. Also take time to ensure you stay as scent-free as possible.*

➤ *When scouting and deciphering a rub line, don't think in terms of hours. Seldom can you discover a rub line and unravel it in one morning, one day or even several days. I've had rub lines that took me years to unravel.*

➤ *If you find a classic, textbook rub line where it's easy to move almost rub to rub along a trail, bottle the moment and cherish the memory. Such rarities might come along only once in a lifetime.*

If what we've been told and often experienced is true, then white-tailed bucks seldom interact at their rubs or follow their rub lines during the rut. Right? Wrong. I've found that if you stay on top of deer activity during the rut, you'll find times when rutting bucks relate to rubs and rub lines.

Chapter 11

ANTLER RUBS
AND RUTTING BUCKS

Some readers are probably wondering how I can dedicate a full chapter to rubs and rutting bucks. After all, many of us have learned that white-tailed bucks show virtually no relationship with their rubs and rub lines during the rut. Heck, everyone knows big-buck travel along rub lines screeches to a halt when the first does enter estrus. We also know bucks won't resume traveling along their rub lines until after the last doe is bred.

That's the way it has always been, right? No. That's not the way it has always been. In fact, I've discovered in recent years that rutting bucks will relate to rubs. I also know of several cases where big bucks were seen moving along their rub lines during the peak of the rut. Granted, some special circumstances existed in almost every one of these instances. Regardless, big bucks sometimes follow their rub lines during the rut.

Big bucks occasionally return to their core areas during the rut. After lying low a day or so, a buck will get into a hectic feeding pattern. Rub-line activity picks up at this time. Once "recharged," bucks quickly resume rut-related pursuits.

My son, Jake, shows off the massive 10-pointer he shot along a rub line during a recent hunt in Wisconsin. The buck was definitely still in a strong rutting mode, proving that rub lines aren't always poor places to hunt during the rut.

From the first day I began sharing my thoughts on rubs and rub lines I've advised against hunting them during the rut. I've also errantly stated that concentrations of rubs are almost always made during the pre-rut. Obviously, I said, you won't catch a big buck near that sign once the rut begins. Man, was I off base on that!

Rutting Bucks and Rub Lines

One special circumstance involving the rut and rub lines concerns antlerless deer numbers. The more breeding-age does in an area, the less big bucks must travel. And the less traveling they do during the rut, the more time they spend in their core areas. This scenario will result in rutting-buck activity along rub lines.

The opposite occurs in areas where antlerless deer numbers are relatively low. This is more common in the big-woods areas I hunt. Because of the scarcity of breeding-age does, big-woods bucks travel extensively during the rut. Little of that travel occurs along active rub lines. Unfortunately, I applied that tendency across the whitetail's vast range.

Contrary to long-held beliefs, rubs can help you zero in on rutting buck activity. Fresh rubs near the edge of a soybean field put me onto this 8-pointer. I lured him into range by placing a buck decoy 20 yards in front of my stand.

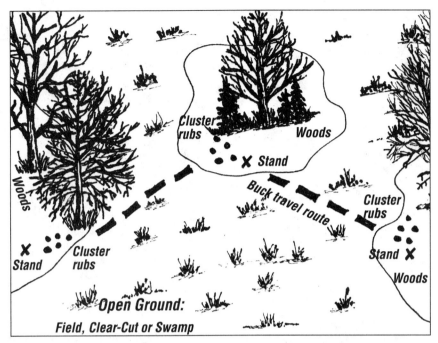

Rutting bucks sometimes relate to rubs and rub lines. But they also relate to "cluster rubs." Look for cluster rubs near points of cover that jut into open areas. Bucks often travel on direct lines to these sites when they're cruising the woods looking for receptive does. Cluster rubs often mark these sites as a buck "connects the dots" in his travels.

Having said that, I have also come to believe hunters everywhere can expect to see some big-buck activity along rub lines during the rut. Why? Several times in recent years I've seen and heard of big bucks returning to their core areas during the peak of the rut. They didn't return to search for hot does, either. Rather, I believe they came home for much-needed rest. They laid low awhile, then spent a day or two feeding ravenously. After replenishing their energy supplies, they jumped back into the breeding game.

When rutting bucks return home to rest, rub-line hunting can suddenly become productive. That's because, just like during the pre-rut, bucks are again traveling rub lines that link bedding and feeding areas.

Of course, before you can hope to exploit this behavior, you first must know when a big buck has returned to his core area. That's not as difficult as you might think. In fact, it's possible you might see a big buck walking around in his core area during the rut. On other occa-

Don't ignore fresh rubs you find near field edges during the rut. Such sign could indicate bucks are regularly visiting the field, either to feed themselves or to check for estrous does that are there to feed.

sions, you must study sign to figure out if a big buck has returned home.

I monitor some rub lines in my areas throughout the rut. If fresh rubs appear along a rub line, or if existing rubs look like they've been reworked, I immediately hunt the rub line. Remember, when a rutting buck returns to rest, he usually sticks around only a couple of days. If you suspect a rub line is being used during the rut, hunt it right away!

Tail-End Action

Another time it's possible to catch a rutting buck on his core-area rub lines is at the tail end of the rut. Big bucks often return home before the rut is "officially" over. It's not that they aren't in a rutting mood, it's just that their energy is drained. Instead of resting and recuperating just anywhere, big bucks almost always return to their core areas. Once home, they'll again start traveling along their rub lines.

At the tail end of the rut, big bucks often return home before the rut is "officially" over because their energy is drained. Once home, they'll again start traveling along their rub lines.

My son, Jake, exploited this situation during a recent gun season. I had placed Jake's portable stand 12 feet up a lone tamarack. The tree stood in the middle of a long, narrow grass swamp bordered on both sides by thick tag alder brush.

Two rub lines were within rifle range of the stand. One of the rub lines ran along the edge of the tag alders on the far edge of the swamp. The other coursed through the tag alders behind Jake's stand. Our hunting partner, Kevin Shibilski, had scouted this area, and had assured us the bucks that made the rub lines were bedded within 100 yards of Jake's tamarack.

Jake's morning hunt was uneventful, but late in the afternoon on opening day he heard a pig-like grunt to his left. He looked that way and was surprised to see a huge buck standing in the middle of the swamp 100 yards away.

As Jake told me later: "I raised my .270 and found the buck in the scope, but I couldn't hold the cross-hairs steady, so I decided not to shoot. The buck stood in the grass for a while, and then walked into a clump of tag alders. I could still hear him grunting, and could tell he was walking my way. But the brush was so thick I could only see parts of him."

Just about the time Jake thought he wouldn't get a shot, he saw a small opening in front of the buck.

"I found the buck in the scope again and followed him until he walked into the opening," he said. "I made sure the cross-hairs were where they belonged and squeezed the trigger. The buck kicked out his hind legs and took off through the tag alders. He went out of sight pretty quick, but I thought I heard him fall."

Jake's 130-grain bullet took the massive 10-pointer through the heart.

As we discovered over the next several days, some rutting activity was still going on, but the rut was definitely winding down. If we had followed old-school beliefs, Jake never would have been sitting in that tamarack. Judging by the buck's swollen neck, his stained hocks, his

For years I struggled with the seemingly unpredictable behavior of rutting bucks. Then I discovered that big bucks like this one continue to make and revisit certain sign throughout the rut.

"I found the buck in the scope and followed him until he walked into the opening ... and squeezed the trigger. The buck kicked out his hind legs and took off into the tag alders."
— *Jake Miller*

strong smell and his general demeanor, Jake's 10-pointer was still much in the rutting mode.

Feeding-Area Rubs

As we've discussed earlier, bucks love to rub near the edges of feeding areas during the pre-rut. Bucks continue to rub near these edges throughout the rut. Not until recently, however, did I discover how to use feeding-area rubs to find productive stands for the rut.

While scouting after a morning hunt one day, I found a "hidden" soybean field. A perimeter check turned up nearly a dozen rubs. I assumed they had been made during the pre-rut, but when I spot-checked the field again several days later, I found several fresh rubs among the ones I noticed earlier. Obviously, the bucks were still visiting the bean field, probably to check the many antlerless deer feeding there every evening. And when they visited the field, they made rubs.

I immediately made new hunting plans. Unfortunately, wind conditions meant I needed to place my stand 75 yards from the largest concentration of buck sign. I knew the stand site would put me out of bow range from where antlerless deer were entering the beanfield. I wasn't comfortable putting all my faith in a grunt call and rattling antlers to lure a big buck into range. Therefore, I placed a buck decoy in the beanfield 20 yards in front of my stand, and faced it toward me.

I had been on my stand about 30 minutes when a doe trotted into the field, stopped and stared at her back-trail. I barely had time to stand when I heard a crash in the timber behind the doe. The next thing I knew, a big buck was standing near the field edge, and he had obviously spotted my decoy. He studied the bogus deer several seconds, grunted loudly and deliberately walked toward me in a stiff-legged gait. The trophy buck quickly closed to 25 yards before stopping and giving the decoy a hard stare. Seconds later he grunted again, laid back his ears and edged toward the decoy in a sidling, hair-flared shuffle. I let him get within 15 yards before sending an arrow through his chest.

The buck closed to 25 yards before stopping and giving the decoy a hard stare. He grunted, laid back his ears and sidled toward the decoy in a hair-flared shuffle. I let him get within 15 yards before sending an arrow through his chest.

Remember, that experience began when I found fresh rubs while scouting during the rut. Rutting bucks constantly prowl near the edges of feeding areas used by antlerless deer. They do this to visually and scent-check the feeding areas for estrous does. While walking the edges of feeding areas, bucks occasionally rub and maybe even scrape.

This rubbing serves myriad purposes. First, it helps bucks release pent up aggression. Second, it helps them pump up their neck muscles even more. And third, it enables them to leave behind calling cards, announcing their presence to bucks and does alike.

For hunters, these rubs can show exactly which food sources attract the most rutting buck activity.

Rut "Cluster" Rubs

Cluster rubs are the easiest of all rut-related rubs to distinguish. That's because they don't show up until the rut kicks in. This timing is what differentiates cluster rubs from rubs marking staging areas. Setting up near cluster rubs can be a productive rut-hunting strategy.

Allow me to explain some facts about cluster rubs and where to find them. As most hunters know, mature bucks seldom follow established trails during the rut. They usually cut directly from one site to another in a "connect-the-dots" routine. It appears big bucks know the shortest distance between these pre-selected sites is a straight line. That explains why it's common to see large bucks traveling across open spaces during the rut. They're simply taking the shortest possible route to reach their destinations.

I struggled with these seemingly random movements for years. How could I hunt big bucks that seldom used established trails? Then I discovered rutting bucks often left clusters of rubs and scrapes at each of their destination points. Even more interestingly, I discovered they routinely visited these clusters throughout the rut.

OK, so where can you expect to find cluster rubs? One of the most obvious places is near road crossings. Interestingly, nothing funnels

Because of their nomadic wanderings during the rut, it's possible to go several days during the rut without seeing a big buck. It's also possible that every buck in the area could walk by your stand in a matter of minutes. You just never know unless you're there to watch.

In the big woods, search for clusters on points of cover jutting into young clear-cuts. Big-woods bucks also tend to make cluster rubs on points of wooded high ground that extend into swamps.

rutting buck movement quite like road crossings. In fact, some of the largest bucks killed each year fall to cars and trucks, and most of these crashes occur during the rut.

Most hunters already know the location of well-used road crossings in their hunting areas. Just make sure you always set up at least the legal distance from the road.

Another good place to find cluster rubs is near points of cover. In agricultural areas, I often find cluster rubs on points of timber that jut into crop lands. And in the big woods, I search for clusters on points of cover jutting into young clear-cuts. Big-woods bucks also tend to make cluster rubs on points of wooded high ground that extend into swamps.

Then again, I also find cluster rubs at seemingly random spots. While some spots are certainly more attractive to cluster-rubbing, I never know without doubt where rutting bucks will make this sign. That's why I constantly try to keep in touch with deer activity wherever I hunt.

A Hit-and-Miss Proposition?

While setting up near cluster rubs can be a productive rut-hunting strategy, nothing is a sure bet. Because of a buck's nomadic searchings during the rut, it's possible to go several days without seeing activity. I maintain a positive attitude through deer-less times by remembering it's entirely possible every big buck in the area could walk by within bow range in a matter of minutes. That's just the way things often go at this time of year.

I once believed that trying to kill big bucks during the rut was a hit-and-miss proposition, at best. But then, contrary to that long-held belief, I discovered that rutting bucks do relate to rubs and that they occasionally travel along their rub-lines.

Applying that knowledge toward my rut hunts has brought a marked improvement in my big-buck success rate.

Greg's Practical Points

➤ *The more breeding-age does in an area, the less big bucks must travel. And the more time big bucks spend in their core areas, the more you'll see them traveling along rub lines.*

➤ *Hunters everywhere can expect to see some big-buck activity along rub lines during the rut. Why? Big bucks sometimes return to their core areas during the peak of the rut.*

➤ *If fresh rubs appear along a rub line, or if existing rubs look like they've been reworked, immediately hunt the rub line! If the buck that made the rub is "home" resting during the rut, he won't stay long.*

➤ *Rutting bucks prowl near the edges of feeding areas used by antlerless deer. They do this to visually and scent-check the areas for estrous does. These rubs can show exactly which food sources attract the most rutting buck activity.*

➤ *Mature bucks seldom follow established trails during the rut. They usually cut directly from one site to another in a "connect-the-dots" routine. They often make cluster rubs at these sites.*

➤ *A good place to find cluster rubs is near points of cover that jut into agricultural fields or recently clear-cut woods.*

Many weeks of hunting pressure usually cause the post-rut deer herd to be highly suspicious and extremely flighty. Big bucks seem to drop off the face of the earth at this time of year.

Chapter 12

HUNTING RUB LINES IN THE POST-RUT

Even though the early season can test hunters' patience and knowledge as they search for rub lines, more hunters seem to prefer this time over the post-rut period. They seem more willing to endure warm temperatures, limited visibility and few fresh rubs, which are just some of the factors that make early-season rub-line hunting difficult.

Much of this eagerness to hunt the early season might be attributed to our long off-season. Hunters just can't wait to get back into the woods to hunt. But it also might be because the deer themselves are coming through their own off-season. In the early season they're still relatively relaxed.

By the time deer reach the late fall and post-rut, however, the cumulative effect of many weeks of hunting pressure puts deer

Big bucks often lie low during the first part of the pre-rut. Once they've restored some of their energy, they indulge in active feeding patterns.

into a suspicious and flighty state. This can make for discouraging hunts. More than anything, though, it's the lifestyles bucks adopt during the post-rut that keeps most hunters home watching football.

Why I Love the Post-Rut

Call me crazy, but I enjoy hunting for big bucks during the post rut. Why? First, most of my post-rut hunts occur where there's snow. As many Northern deer hunters know, snow always makes it easier to scout for and locate big bucks. Second, seldom must I worry

Fresh or reworked rubs can tell you exactly which rub lines are being used by post-rut bucks. In some cases, these will be the same rub lines used earlier in the year to connect bedding and feeding areas.

about interference from other hunters. Once I locate a big deer, I usually have him all to myself. And that's always a huge advantage!

Then again, when I was developing my post-rut hunting skills, I had no choice in the matter. Much of my deer hunting revolved around the post-rut, whether I liked it or not. You see, just about every year I deal with post-rut situations during Wisconsin's gun-deer season. It's also a given that deer display post-rut tendencies throughout the late archery season. Therefore, I realized long ago that I had to learn a lot about post-rut buck behavior.

But make no mistake. The importance of learning rub-line deer behavior in the post-rut isn't unique to Wisconsin deer hunters. These days, it seems nearly every state has a rifle,

Successful hunts during the post-rut period often depend on placing your stands close to a buck's bedding area. If you were hunting and scouting these areas in the pre-rut, you already should have some stands picked out for the post-rut. Be sure you can reach these stands without creating any disturbance.

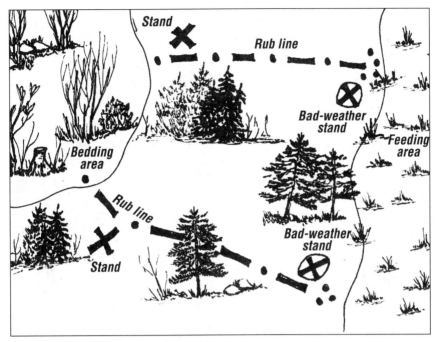

Don't totally rule out rub-line stands for hunting near feeding areas. Remember that big-buck activity near feeding areas will increase dramatically shortly before bouts of arctic cold blasts or winter storms.

shotgun, muzzleloader or archery season during at least part of the post-rut. As a result, finding, deciphering and hunting post-rut rub lines can benefit deer hunters across North America.

Understanding Post-Rut Behavior

Let's discuss some vital aspects of post-rut deer behavior. For a month or longer, bucks put far more effort into finding and breeding receptive does than they do on eating. As a result, an active breeding buck can lose 30 percent of his body weight during the rut. Because nature's law dictates only the strongest survive, it's imperative that bucks resume feeding as soon as possible after the rut. They must restore their depleted fat supplies as much as possible, especially in areas with severe winters.

Big bucks are among the first deer to die in severe Northern winters. With little fat from which to draw energy, bucks weaken in deep snow and sub-zero temperatures. They often die of stress or get singled out and killed by coyotes or wolves.

Post-rut bucks often use the same travel routes they used during the pre-rut. If you were scouting earlier in the fall, you should know of some rub-line "ends" near bedding areas. At the same time, you should have picked and prepared some stand sites near those hotspots.

Michigan's John Ozoga, research editor for *Deer & Deer Hunting* magazine, is a well-known deer authority. We talked a couple of years ago about the white-tailed buck's physiology during the post-rut.

"Big bucks that have been busy chasing and breeding for four to five weeks will lie low for part of the post-rut," Ozoga told me. "Once the bucks get their legs under them again, they'll get into pretty active feeding patterns."

Is locating prime food sources the only prerequisite for post-rut success? On occa-

This heavy-beamed 8-pointer followed a rub line to the alfalfa field where I was set up. A blast of brutally cold arctic air put the post-rut buck into a daytime feeding pattern.

sion it's that simple. In most cases, though, ambushing a post-rut trophy entails far more than knowing "hot" deer-feeding areas. You also need a basic understanding of how big bucks relate to their rubs and rub lines at this time.

Finding Productive Post-Rut Rub Lines

The best place to start post-season rub-line scouting is — no surprise here — feeding areas. And again, the best way to find active rub lines is by walking the feeding areas' perimeters. By the time the post-rut arrives, bucks will have been working their rub lines at least two months, which means lots of rubs will be in the woods. As a result, it shouldn't take long to figure out which routes are seeing the most use. Fresh and reworked rubs are dead giveaways.

The daily bedding and travel routines of post-rut bucks are

I believe mature bucks are more sensitive to human presence during the post-rut than at any other time of the hunting season. You can't make any mistakes if you want them to come close enough for a shot.

dictated largely by food sources. However, when scouting for rub-line stands, you can't just set up anywhere along a rub line and expect success. Heck, there's no guarantee you'll even see post-rut activity. Mature bucks are notorious for waiting until last light before leaving their bedding areas. You can bet these deer will also slip back into their daytime hideouts at first light. Therefore, the closer you can set up to bedding areas, the greater your chances for success.

How can you do the necessary scouting and stand-site preparation without tipping your hand to nearby big bucks? Good question, but it shouldn't be too difficult. Post-rut bucks often use the same travel routes (rub lines) they used during the pre-rut. If you were scouting earlier in the fall, you should know of some rub-line "ends" near bedding areas. At the same time, you should have picked and prepared some stand sites near those hotspots.

Of course, there will always be times when early-fall scouting wasn't possible, or you decide to hunt elsewhere in the post-rut. Obviously, because post-rut bucks are in a delicate frame of mind, you don't want to stomp all over the landscape searching for productive rub-line stands.

Here's what I do: I start by placing my post-rut stands along likely looking rub lines about 75 to 100 yards from the edge of

Certain weather factors can prompt even the most nocturnal post-rut bucks to move in daylight. Simply put, the worse the weather, the better the rub-line hunting.

feeding areas. I then make a couple of hunts from these spots, and decide if I should stay or move. If I'm seeing big-buck activity and I'm confident one of them will eventually walk by within range, I stay. But if I'm not seeing bucks, I move deeper into the woods. I keep moving inward until I see some buck activity or dare not move any closer to a suspected bedding area.

I have two options if I don't see any buck activity from the last spot. I move to a new area or wait until conditions favor daytime buck activity before hunting the spot again.

Watch the Weather

Certain weather factors can prompt even the most nocturnal post-rut bucks to move in daylight. Simply put, the worse the weather, the better the rub-line hunting.

Whitetails become more active in the 12 hours before a major winter storm arrives. The activity starts as a trickle and continues to grow as the storm nears. In the final hours before the storm hits, whitetails, including big bucks, often head for the nearest food. Interestingly, the time of day doesn't matter. The deer will fill their bellies before conditions turn nasty.

I once arrowed a monster nontypical during Wisconsin's late archery season. An approaching storm prompted him to abandon his nocturnal travel patterns. Unbelievably, he followed one of his rub lines and stepped into the alfalfa field a half-hour before dark. A perfect hit at 15 yards ended my two-year quest for this record-book 18-pointer.

Severe, sudden temperature drops can also prompt post-rut whitetails into daylight activity. A couple of seasons after I got my 18-pointer, I arrowed another big buck when a sudden blast of brutal arctic air spurred deer into hectic feeding patterns. Just as the nontypical had done, the heavy-antlered 8-pointer followed a rub line to reach a snow-covered alfalfa field. I had

The heavy-antlered 8-pointer followed a rub line to reach a snow-covered alfalfa field. I had to wait until he stepped clear of several antlerless deer before shooting. The buck ran about 100 yards before going down for good.

to wait until he stepped clear of several antlerless deer before shooting. The buck ran about 100 yards before going down for good.

Sometimes Things Don't Work Out

Not all of my post-rut hunts have such happy endings. One year I was posted along a rub line when a monster buck walked out of a thick tangle of prickly ash about 75 yards away. After scoping the area for several minutes, he started heading my way.

He closed to 30 yards when things suddenly went sour. The trophy whitetail somehow knew something wasn't right. He stood in one spot, looking, listening and sniffing for nearly 15 minutes. I didn't move a muscle or make a sound the entire time, and the wind was in my favor. Still, the buck knew something was wrong. He stayed put a few more minutes, and then flicked his tail and disappeared back into the prickly ash. I never saw him again.

Unfortunately, that disappointment isn't the only one I've known in the late season. The same thing has happened on several other post-rut hunts. In fact, I clearly remember three other big bucks that somehow detected me and then walked away unscathed.

Can I explain those poor results? I almost swear that post-rut bucks can "feel" predatory threats. By the time the post-rut rolls around, big bucks have experienced so much hunting pressure that their senses have been honed to an extremely keen edge.

While deer are always concerned about human activities, I think big bucks are most sensitive to it during the post-rut. You simply can't make any mistakes! If you even suspect deer have caught on to your plan, leave the area alone a few days. Don't

Learning how to deal with post-rut bucks has paid big dividends for me during Wisconsin's firearms deer seasons.

Some big bucks refuse to move on their own in daylight. My gun-hunting partners and I have found a way to "induce" these bucks to leave their beds and travel along their rub lines during shooting hours. How? We post two hunters downwind on rub lines, and then send in another hunter or two upwind of the bedding area.

return unless all conditions, especially wind direction, are fully in your favor.

Post-Rut Bucks Under the Gun

Where should you sit if gun-hunting the post-rut? If my experiences are any indication, I want my rub-line stands very near bedding areas. The sudden intrusion of humans into every corner of deer range will drive post-rut bucks deeply into reclusive, daylight-shy lifestyles. Unless you're set up almost within sight of where bucks are bedding, it's doubtful you'll get a glimpse of them during the season.

Wisconsin's gun season, for example, almost always opens during the post-rut. Nothing I've learned about post-rut hunting for skittish deer proves as crucial and helpful as posting near bedding areas. Two examples come to mind. The first involves a big-woods buck I discovered just days before the gun season opened. The buck had finished his rutting duties and was again living in his core area. At first I thought I would be able to ambush him anywhere along one of his active rub lines. By the third day of the season, I realized my judgment error.

Fortunately, I found the buck's bedding area and the end of an active rub line at the edge of the bedding area. I prepared a

I found the buck's bedding area and the end of an active rub line at the edge of the bedding area. I prepared a stand, and shot the buck shortly before shooting time ended the next afternoon.

stand, and shot the buck shortly before shooting time ended the next afternoon. I doubt he was more than five yards from the edge of his bedding area when I squeezed the trigger on my .270.

I had a similar experience with another big-woods buck three years later. I had hunted the deer off and on since opening day, and it was now the morning of Day 5. My stand was on the northern edge of a small spruce swamp where I suspected the buck was bedding. Several rub lines coursed into the thick spruce, but the only buck activity I had seen was a small 6-point buck.

My fortune changed dramatically two hours after daylight. A flicker of movement near the swamp's edge caught my eye. I turned to see a large-racked whitetail walking slowly away. I raised my rifle, centered the buck in the cross-hairs, and waited for a better angle. Seconds later, the buck turned just enough. I instantly sent a 130-grain missile through the 11-pointer's vitals.

Like I said, it's important for gun-hunters to set up near bedding areas during the post-rut.

Some Last-Ditch Post-Rut Strategies

Let's discuss some other post-rut tactics to try. I've found, for example, that it's sometimes possible to coax nocturnal bucks out of their bedding areas. Your stand sites, however, must be on active rub lines near buck bedding areas. It's also imperative that you slip into those stands without the least bit of disturbance.

If used right, rattling and grunting can be effective in the post-rut. The key is to make a subtle presentation. You merely want to pique a bedded buck's curiosity. Bring the rattling antlers together gently and lightly tickle the tines. When trying a grunt call, blow on it softly several times and then put it

---

I prefer to sit quietly on my post-rut stands and trust natural deer movement along the rub line to bring a buck within range. Rattling, grunting and forced-movement strategies are last resorts.

---

away. Don't expect post-rut bucks to charge out of their bedding areas to check for intruders. They'll more likely take a slow, deliberate approach.

My gun-hunting partners and I use another strategy for dealing with nocturnal, post-rut bucks. A couple of hunters sneak into the woods and set up on active rub lines on the downwind side of a bedding area. At a prearranged time, one or two of us walks to the upwind side of the bedding area and moseys around. We might even slowly walk a little way into the bedding area.

Our intent is to have the bedded bucks smell the upwind intruders, abandon their beds, and head out along one of the rub lines to a waiting hunter. This tactic works often enough to warrant a try on uncooperative bucks.

Even so, I prefer to sit quietly on my post-rut stands and trust natural deer movement along the rub line to bring a buck within range. My hunting partners and I try rattling, grunting and forced-movement strategies only as last resorts.

Give it a Try

While it's true you should expect more adversity during the post-rut than at any other time, this can be a productive time to kill a big buck. It merely requires you analyze the situation and adjust your plans accordingly. The greatest adjustments involve establishing stands where you can take advantage of the little bit of daylight wandering big bucks do at this time of year.

Again, when I consider all the possible ways to hunt the post-rut, I find rub lines are the best alternative.

Greg's Practical Points

➤ *Hunters seldom need to worry about interference from other hunters during the post-rut. Once you locate a big deer at this time, you'll usually have him all to yourself.*

➤ *Learning rub-line deer behavior in the post-rut is helpful wherever you hunt. Nearly every state has a firearms or archery season during part of the post-rut.*

➤ *In most cases, ambushing a post-rut trophy entails more than knowing "hot" feeding areas. You also need to understand how big bucks relate to their rubs and rub lines.*

➤ *Mature bucks often wait until last light before leaving their bedding areas. You can bet they will also slip back into their daytime hideouts at first light. The closer you can set up to bedding areas, the greater your chances for success.*

➤ *When placing post-rut stands, start along likely looking rub lines about 75 to 100 yards from the edge of feeding areas. Make two hunts before deciding whether to move.*

➤ *Big bucks are most sensitive to human activity during the post-rut. You simply can't make any mistakes!*

➤ *It's sometimes possible to coax nocturnal bucks out of their bedding areas if you lightly rattle or grunt-call from active rub lines near a buck's bedding area.*

The more bucks living within the same core area, the more rub and scrape sign you will find in staging areas.

Chapter 13

HUNTING A BUCK'S STAGING AREAS

One aspect of rub-related behavior that seems to have fallen by the hunters' wayside in recent years is buck staging areas. As recently as the mid-1990s, deer hunters commonly knew and talked about staging areas. In fact, the terms *rub line* and *staging area* seemed to be linked in popularity. Hunters seldom mentioned one without the other.

By the late 1990s, however, I rarely heard other hunters discuss staging areas. I don't know why the term became so rare. It could be that many of today's newer hunters simply haven't heard of staging areas, or maybe the experienced hunters don't believe staging areas exist.

Let me assure you, staging areas exist. What are they? In brief, staging areas are semi-open areas within thick cover where bucks can "stage" while waiting for darkness to cover their entry into nearby fields to feed or cross. While waiting in staging areas, which are

I found this staging area while hunting for coyotes. It seems few deer hunters understand the important role staging areas can play in the pre-rut rituals of white-tailed bucks. These sites can be hotspots if you don't overhunt them.

usually found about 100 to 150 yards back into the woods, bucks often rub and scrape.

Don't assume the information in this chapter doesn't apply in your area. Over the past 13 years I've been able to hunt whitetails across a broad swath of North America. If I've learned one thing from all those hunts, it's that some aspects of buck behavior remain constant regardless of the region. This is never more true than with staging areas.

I'm sure just about everyone who has spent some time hunting whitetails has seen at least one staging area. Some hunters I talk with say they've seen several. I suspect most hunters have seen staging areas, but didn't know what they were looking at. Sadly, those guys don't have a clue about the significant role staging areas play in a buck's pre-rut rituals. If they did, they would know that setting up near staging areas can be productive during the pre-rut.

Identifying Staging Areas

Staging areas are easy to identify. In almost every case, you'll find good numbers of rubs concentrated in a relatively small area. The rubs

This clover field was attracting many whitetails. I found several staging areas in thicker cover back in from the field edge.

There's some chance you'll catch a buck near an open feeding area in daylight. Your chances for a big buck are greater, however, near staging areas.

might be on trees, saplings, clumps of brush or all three. The number of rubs will vary between staging areas. Of course, a buck's temperament is a big factor. Some bucks just aren't as rub-active as others. Some bucks seem to rub several different trees, saplings and/or bushes each time they visit their staging areas. In addition, bucks often establish a number of scrapes in conjunction with their staging areas.

Another factor that can have a huge bearing on rub numbers is the number of bucks visiting a staging area. As with all rubs, it's common behavior for every buck in the locale to repeatedly work the same staging areas. The more bucks sharing a core area, the more rub activity you can expect in their staging areas.

Staging areas don't come in standard sizes. I've found some sprawled for many yards in every direction, while others measure a mere 15 yards in diameter. As is often times the case with rub numbers, a staging area's size can be dictated by several factors, including terrain, buck numbers and time of year. One thing remains constant, however. Your chances for success are higher when hunting around slightly smaller staging areas. I'll explain why a bit later in this chapter.

Like rub lines, bucks establish staging areas in early fall, and they continue to visit these "playgrounds" throughout the pre-rut. The visits become more frequent and take place in daylight more often as the pre-rut progresses. This increase in daylight activity peaks just before the rut. Buck activity at staging areas drops sharply once breeding begins.

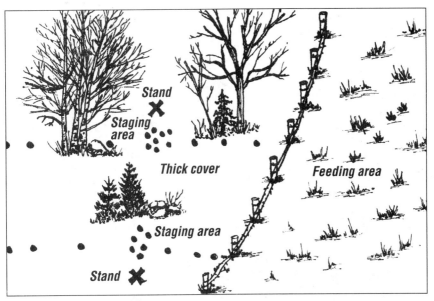

Bucks often establish staging areas within thick cover about 50 to 100 yards from the edge of feeding areas. While mature bucks seldom go near food sources in open fields until after dark, they sometimes can be caught "working out" in staging areas in daylight.

Finding Staging Areas

If you can find active rub lines, you should be able to find some staging areas. Most staging areas are located along rub lines. But while it's possible to find them anywhere along rub lines, bucks seem to favor certain spots over others. One of these spots is in heavier cover back a ways from the edges of feeding areas. Another common spot is in thick cover near open crossing points. In almost every instance, at least one rub line will lead to these types of staging areas.

Staging areas back from the edge of feeding areas are the easiest to find and hunt. Besides the fact they're almost always found along active rub lines, they're seldom more than 100 yards from the edge of feeding areas. Even if you can't find an active rub line, you should be able to find these kinds of staging areas. An effective strategy I use is to walk 50 yards straight into the woods from the edge of a feeding area. Then turn right or left and walk all the way around the feeding area. If you don't find anything on your first pass, go 50 yards farther into the woods and make another circuit. Continue this routine until you find some staging areas or until you're about 200 yards from the feeding areas. More times than not, by the time I'm finished with this

Whether you want to believe it or not, the areas you now hunt contain staging areas. Staging areas are always found along rub lines. If you don't overhunt them, you'll be hard-pressed to find more productive areas during the pre-rut.

scouting, I'll have found several staging areas.

You can also pinpoint staging areas by simply paying attention while sitting on your evening stands. Bucks, especially mature animals, make a lot of noise while working out in their staging areas. They rub trees, thrash brush, break branches and throw leaves and dirt while working scrapes. Big bucks often grunt loudly while performing those rituals. Provided the wind doesn't play tricks on your ears, you should be able to pinpoint the sounds' location. Wait until the middle part of the next day to search for the staging area.

Why Bucks Establish Staging Areas

I believe bucks establish staging areas because of their aversion to open places in daylight. While does, fawns and immature bucks often appear in open feeding areas long before dark, mature bucks are seldom so carefree. For most of the season they won't show up at feeding areas until after dark. That doesn't mean they never move in daylight. I've seen a bunch of big-buck activity during shooting hours, with much of it occurring near staging areas.

Almost all staging areas are located along rub lines. However, bucks establish staging areas only where they feel safe and secure.

As with other aspects of rub behavior, bucks again relate to staging areas during the post-rut. Don't abandon them for good when the rut kicks in.

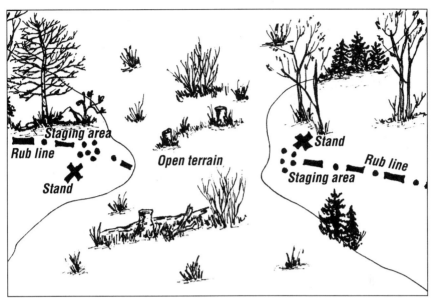

Staging areas might also be found within thick cover near open-ground crossing points. Mature bucks usually hang back in thick cover and "stage" until darkness falls, and then cross the opening when they feel safe.

I remember one of my first experiences in a staging area. I had discovered the hotspot while in-season scouting about 150 yards from the edge of a lush alfalfa field. The staging area held a bonanza of buck sign. At least two dozen fresh rubs were scattered about a clearing. In addition, a row of steaming scrapes followed one edge of the clearing. I prepared a tree for my portable stand, and then sneaked away.

The first time I hunted that stand near the staging area was a week later. Unbelievably, I arrowed a beautiful 10-point buck less than 15 minutes after settling in. I have no doubt the alfalfa field was the buck's destination.

Unfortunately for him, he made the fatal mistake of visiting his staging area first. Judging by the amount of fresh sign, this was a daily routine for the buck. Given his pace, there's no way he would have arrived at the alfalfa field before dark.

That buck reinforced a couple of important points about staging areas. First, while big bucks often avoid feeding areas in daylight, they don't seem as hesitant about visiting their in-woods "playgrounds." Second, the absolute best time to hunt near staging areas is during the late pre-rut.

Don't overhunt staging-area stands. Even young bucks won't tolerate constant intrusions. Bucks establish several staging areas, so set up near a different one every time you hunt.

Crossing-Point Staging Areas

I mentioned earlier that bucks often establish staging areas near open-area crossing points. The reason, as with feeding areas, is that antlerless deer and young bucks often won't hesitate to cross open ground in daylight. Big bucks will seldom do that except during the rut. Although a mature buck might reach an open-area crossing point before dark, he'll seldom cross right away. Most likely, he will hang back in the cover and await darkness. What does he do while waiting? He "stages." He rubs his antlers on trees and bushes, makes new scrapes and freshens old ones. It takes only a couple of these sessions to establish an obvious staging area near the crossing.

As with staging areas they establish near feeding areas, big bucks become most active in daylight near crossing-point staging areas during the final days of the pre-rut. That doesn't mean you should stay away until the late pre-rut. In fact, I encourage you to sit these stands throughout the season. But whatever you do, don't overhunt staging-area stands. Even young bucks won't tolerate constant intrusions to the same spot.

There's an easy, effective way to avoid this mistake. Almost without exception, bucks establish several staging areas throughout their range. Therefore, you can set up near one staging area for your first hunt, and then set up near a different one the next. After that, you can wait near yet another of a buck's staging areas. That allows you to hunt the same buck three days in a row, but always from a different stand. Provided you hunt only when the wind favors a particular stand, and provided you keep disturbances to a minimum, this strategy works.

Staging Areas and Buck Bedrooms

Bucks also establish staging areas near the outside edges of their bedding areas. These are the most active and potentially productive staging areas. The problem is, they're also the most difficult to find and hunt. In fact, unless you took time during the off-season to pinpoint staging areas near bedding areas and prepare stand sites, don't go near them. Bucks usually bed so close to these sites that it's impossible to prepare stand sites without being detected. While it's OK to cause disturbances in or near buck bedding areas during the off-season, it's not wise during the season.

If finding bed-related staging areas is so tough, why do I bring it up? Well, like I said, these staging areas are the most active and potentially productive of all. If you take time during the off-season to locate one or two of these staging areas, you could be set for an incredible string of

Mature bucks are often extremely cautious when approaching staging areas. They quickly leave if they suspect a threat.

successes. If you're set up so close to where big bucks are resting, success could come any time during the season, including the dreaded October lull! That alone is enough to prod most hunters into some off-season scouting for staging areas.

More on Staging Areas

In my early days of rub-line hunting, I sometimes couldn't figure out why a buck established a staging area in a certain spot. I couldn't find a good food source nearby, and the nearest open ground was a good distance away. After a lot of scouting and firsthand observations, I finally found an answer.

I think certain places along rub lines make big bucks feel more secure. Maybe a spot is surrounded by thick brush. Or maybe it provides great visibility of the surroundings. Whatever the reason, bucks not only feel comfortable approaching the spot, but they also feel safe enough to lower their guard for some serious rubbing and scraping.

When big bucks focus on rubbing or scraping, they can become nearly oblivious to their surroundings. Wait for a buck to start rubbing or scraping before drawing your bow.

When big bucks become focused on serious rubbing or scraping, they can become nearly oblivious to their surroundings. If you wait for a buck to start rubbing or scraping before drawing your bow or getting positioned for a shot, you stand little chance of getting picked off.

There is a down side to hunting near staging areas, however. I think mature bucks are aware they're vulnerable while rubbing or scraping. I believe that's why they're so cautious when approaching staging areas. If they suspect a threat might exist, they quickly depart. When hunting near staging areas, be careful or deal with the consequences!

Once the rut arrives and staging areas go cold, don't abandon them for the entire season. After the rut, bucks once again relate to staging areas. Obviously then, it's wise during the post-rut to hunt staging areas you previously hunted during the pre-rut.

Go Small, and Know a Staging Area When You See It

I mentioned earlier that it's best to concentrate your efforts around smaller staging areas. The reason should be obvious to bow-hunters. Stand site selection isn't as critical near small staging areas. Let's say you find a staging area roughly 30 yards in diameter. If you place your stand near the center of the staging area, you'll be within effective range of any buck that visits it.

Some hunters say they wouldn't recognize a staging area if they were standing in its middle. If you use a little common sense, you'll recognize them. Anytime you find a lot of rubs and scrapes in a relatively small area, ask yourself, "Could a buck or bucks have made all this sign in just one or two visits?"

If you don't think so, the buck (or bucks) is probably visiting the spot regularly. Congratulations, you've just found a staging area!

Greg's Practical Points —————————

➤ Staging areas are usually found within thick cover where pre-rut or post-rut bucks can "stage" while waiting for darkness to cover their entry into nearby fields to feed or cross. The best time to hunt staging areas is the late pre-rut.

➤ Some aspects of buck behavior remain constant regardless of the region. This is especially true of staging areas. Your favorite woods has staging areas. You might just not realize it.

➤ In almost every case, staging areas can be identified by many rubs and scrapes in a relatively small area. If it looks like it took several visits by bucks to make the rubs and scrapes, it's likely a staging area.

➤ Staging areas don't come in standard sizes. I've found some sprawled for many yards in every direction, while others measure a mere 15 yards in diameter.

➤ Small staging areas are easier to hunt because stand placement isn't as critical. Why? The smaller the area, the easier it is to cover it from one or two stand sites.

➤ Staging areas at the edge of bedding areas are top producers. But if you don't prepare stand sites in the off-season, stay away during the open season.

➤ Most staging areas are 50 to 100 yards from field edges. Walk 50 yards into the woods and circle the feeding area. If you find nothing, move in another 50 yards and make a second circuit.

➤ Bucks establish staging areas because of their aversion to open places in daylight. While does, fawns and immature bucks often appear in open feeding areas long before dark, mature bucks are seldom so carefree.

My brother Jeff poses with a big buck he killed recently. Jeff learned long ago it takes a tremendous amount of effort to consistently shoot bucks like this one.

Chapter 14

SOME FINAL WORDS ON RUB LINES

I can't stress enough how much my success on big white-tailed bucks is attributed to my constant study of rubs and rub lines. Let me be clear, however, that my work and insights into this fascinating aspect of deer hunting aren't unique to me. The knowledge I've amassed could be compiled by anyone who's willing to scout as relentlessly as I do. Likewise, most hunters could enjoy the kind of success I've had if they work hard putting that rub-line knowledge to work.

No doubt you've noticed by now my emphasis on hard work and perseverance. While I'm a big believer in natural ability, I also know the only way to maximize those skills is through diligent work. Other deer hunting "experts" might promise you a world of insights and secrets, but I'll guarantee those tips will do nothing to improve your hunting success unless you're constantly in the woods amassing information about deer

That's me posing by a big rub nearly 14 years before I wrote Rub-Line Secrets. *At the time I wrote this book, I could draw on 20 years of rub-line hunting know-how. Still, I know I haven't learned all there is to know about rubs and rub lines, and I seriously doubt I ever will.*

I'm on a first-name basis with dozens of successful trophy whitetail hunters. Not one of them got where he is today by taking shortcuts. Then again, it's impossible to take something that just isn't there.

where you hunt. So beware of anyone who tells you he knows a shortcut to success. It might work once, but consistent success is seldom easily achieved.

The Harder You Work, the Better You'll Get

Over the past 10 years I've given scores of seminars on the finer points of rub-line hunting. At almost every seminar someone asks how long it took me to figure out my rub-line tactics. I'm sure many people in the audiences are surprised by my answer, and judging by the raised eyebrows and skeptical looks, some of them don't believe me.

The full truth, though, is simple. It took me years to figure out how white-tailed bucks commonly relate to their rubs and rub lines. And I'm totally sincere when I add that I still don't know all there is to know about rubs and rub lines. Further, I doubt I'll ever know all there is to know. Nor will anyone else for that matter. Even so, I hope I'll continue to enjoy a moderate degree of rub-line success.

My son was 13 years old when I took this photo. Even at this young age, Jake knew darn few "classic" rub lines exist. You'll seldom find a rub line where you can just move through the woods from rub to rub connecting the dots.

I suspect too many hunters are obsessed with finding quick fixes for their deer-hunting failures. The sooner you forget about quick fixes and get to work, the sooner you'll enjoy success!

Two specific parts of my answer seem to draw the most surprise and skepticism. The first part concerns how long it took me to "figure out this rub-line thing." For some reason, people struggle to believe I spent many frustrating years studying rub lines before I tasted my first big-buck success. Maybe a lot of hunters don't want to believe it might take them years to hone their own rub-line skills.

I'm troubled at times because I suspect too many hunters are obsessed with finding quick fixes for their deer-hunting failures. Take it from someone who has put a lot of blood, sweat and tears into studying and hunting near rubs and rub lines for trophy whitetail. The sooner you forget about finding a quick fix and get to work, the sooner you'll enjoy some success!

Even more troubling is that the thirst for a quick fix seems to be infecting all aspects of deer hunting, not just rub-line hunting. Many hunters are out there searching for the mythical shortcut, because they're convinced they exist.

I'm on a first-name basis with dozens of successful trophy whitetail hunters. Not one of them got where he is by taking shortcuts. Then again, you can't take something that isn't there. Each one of them has worked extremely hard, and almost single-mindedly, to achieve their success.

Think in Terms of Years, Not Hours

I have my reasons for being so adamant about working hard at rub-line hunting and scouting. Many times in recent years hunters have complained to me about being unable to find, decipher and effectively hunt rub lines. But when I ask how much time they've spent trying to increase their rub-line knowledge, I never hear the word "years." For that matter, I seldom hear the word "weeks." I hear "days" and "hours." You must accept the fact it will take years to acquire the knowledge required to consistently kill mature whitetails as they move along their rub lines.

Why is it such a longtime learning process? Well, no matter how hard you work, or how much scouting you do, it's rare to find many "classic"

I've seen so many big bucks while rub-line hunting that it's impossible to remember them all. Even with all these sightings, however, only a handful of my rub-line hunts resulted in a filled tag. That's just the way it is, but rub-line hunting is still the most consistent, season-long tactic I know of.

looking rub lines. Think back to Chapter 10 in this book. You'll recall I stated that in all my years of scouting, studying and hunting rub lines, I've seen only one example of a classic rub line. These are textbook rub lines where there's almost always another rub within sight of the last one you found.

As I've so painfully found out the past 15-plus years, mature bucks seldom make obvious, easily unraveled rub lines. I go into my rub-line scouting trips expecting it could take at least several days to figure out just a few rub lines. And yes, even with all my years of experience on rub lines, I still get my butt kicked occasionally. Some rub lines are virtually impos-

Some hunters can't resist practice-drawing their bows on small bucks. Although this might seem like a harmless ritual, it can prove costly. Not only might a big buck spot the movement from a distance and start avoiding the area, but you could educate next year's trophy about where you like to hunt.

sible to unravel, and most such rub lines are made by bucks of a unique temperament. However, terrain features can also make some rub lines impossible to unravel.

No Guarantees

One of the largest whitetails I ever hunted constantly gave me the slip. This happened even though I knew where he bedded, where he preferred to feed, and which rub lines he followed between these places. Granted, I hunted this buck fairly often, but I also hunted him carefully. I actually saw him a grand total of one time. He walked within 15 yards of my stand one cold morning late in the pre-rut. Unfortunately, he was nearly covered up by a thick tangle of gray dogwood brush. He eventually

This book can teach you a lot about rub-line hunting, but you hold the key to your own long-term success. The key to becoming a more successful big-buck hunter is to develop an exhausting work ethic for hunting and scouting. And be sure to temper your enthusiasm with caution and common sense.

moved off without offering a shot. The next time I saw him he was lying dead in the back of another hunter's pickup.

Although he was the most memorable buck to beat me, he certainly isn't the only trophy whitetail to accomplish the feat. I've scouted, deciphered and hunted along hundreds of rub lines since about 1980. I've seen more big bucks than I can remember during that time. Still, only a handful of my rub-line hunts resulted in a tagged trophy. That's just the way it is.

Maybe some hunters reading this are thinking the above comment means hunting along rub lines isn't the hot ticket I make it out to be. Maybe not, but I don't know of any big-buck hunting tactic or technique that boasts a high success rate.

In fact, I know of no strategy besides rub-line hunting that remains effective throughout the season. Again, I'm not implying rub-line hunting guarantees success. But I am saying that, over time, it's more productive than anything else out there.

You'll consistently fail if you tromp around your hunting areas too much during the season, or concentrate on one or two rub lines. And never walk into and out of your stands on routes that take you through the heart of deer-activity areas.

Don't Blow It!

Some hunters I know can find and unravel big-buck rub lines. However, they struggle mightily to kill the buck that made the rub lines. At first I couldn't figure out why this always seemed to plague certain hunters. But when I talked with several of them, it didn't take me long to figure out why big bucks refused to walk past their rub-line stands.

For one, they tromp around their hunting areas too much during the season. Next, they concentrate all their hunting on just one or two rub lines. Worse, they walk into and out of their rub-line stands on routes that take them through the heart of deer-activity areas. Unbelievably, a few of them hunted some of their rub-line stands every day of the week!

I've had aspiring rub-line hunters tell me about other costly mistakes. Although all mistakes must eventually be eliminated, one needs to be shot on sight. This involves a ritual some bow-hunters perform nearly every time a doe or small buck walks by their stands. They simply can't resist drawing their bows and counting coup on the deer.

What's the harm in "catch-and-release" bow-hunting? White-tailed bucks often use the same rub lines every year. However, that will stop if bucks detect a threat along a certain rub line. Some of the little bucks you're fooling around with now eventually grow up to be big bucks. If you're not careful, they'll know where you hunt before they grow up.

OK, so maybe you've never been picked off by a small buck while practice-drawing, and you don't see a good reason to stop. Let me tell a story I heard from an Illinois deer hunter. He had been bow-hunting a monster buck for nearly a month. He had seen the buck several times along one rub line early in the season, but then the buck dropped out of sight.

"I was a bit concerned I might have done something wrong," the guy said. "But I was still seeing quite a few immature bucks on the rub line. None of them appeared spooked, so I figured the big buck was still around, but that he just wasn't traveling much in daylight."

He soon found out the hard way that the buck was, indeed, doing some

---

Everything I've written in this book about rubs and rub lines — from off-season scouting to the proper way to hunt rub lines — is exactly the way it is. There's no fluff, no filler, no gimmicks and — most certainly — no shortcuts.

---

daytime traveling.

"I was hunting along the rub line one morning when this small buck showed up," he said. "Instead of just sitting still and letting the buck walk by, I grabbed my bow and made a few practice draws on him. Well, I had just completed my third practice draw when I got this feeling I was being watched. I turned my head slightly and spotted another deer standing on the rub line 20 yards away. It was the monster buck I'd been chasing all fall! He had been watching me practice-draw on the smaller buck. He spun around and took off the second we made eye contact. I never saw him again."

Farewell, and Hunt Hard

I want to say one last thing in closing. Everything I've written in this book about rubs and rub lines — from the importance of off-season scouting to the proper way to hunt rub lines — is exactly the way it is. There's no fluff, no filler, no gimmicks and — most certainly — no shortcuts. I've done my best to give you nothing but my honest observations and frank insights.

Above all, remember that no matter how thoroughly you've read this book, you're the one that holds the key to becoming a more successful big-buck hunter. If you accept the fact you must devote a lot of time and effort to scouting and hunting, this book will help put you in place to ambush a big whitetail. But this book cannot scout and hunt for you, nor instill a healthy work ethic for scouting and hunting. Those things can only come from within you.

With that said, remember to have fun while hunting, and to always temper your enthusiasm with caution and common sense.

I wish you the best of luck on all your rub-line hunts.

Greg's Practical Points ———————————

➤ *Beware anyone who tells you he knows a shortcut to success. It might work once, but consistent success is seldom easily achieved.*

➤ *I spent many frustrating years studying rub lines before I tasted my first big-buck success.*

➤ *When studying and hunting rub lines, don't think you'll become well-versed in hours or days. You need to think in terms of months and years! The sooner you accept this fact, the sooner you'll enjoy success.*

➤ *Mature bucks seldom make obvious, easily unraveled rub lines. I go into my rub-line scouting trips expecting it will take at least several days to figure out just a few rub lines.*

➤ *No strategy besides rub-line hunting remains effective throughout the season. While it can't guarantee success, it's more productive over the long haul than any other strategy.*

➤ *Don't practice-draw on deer. If you aren't going to shoot, don't move. You could alert unseen deer or spook the deer you're drawing on. Either way, you'll risk advertising your presence and ruining the stand.*

➤ *This book cannot scout and hunt for you, nor instill a healthy work ethic for hunting. Those things can only come from within you.*

ABOUT THE ARTWORK

I thought it important to thank my father, Chuck Miller, and Charlie Alsheimer for the unique artwork appearing in this book. My father did the drawings, and Charlie provided the inspiration.

I've been privileged to see many bucks make rubs over the years, and it's fair to say each buck rubs a bit differently than the next. A common misconception is that bucks always rub with the front side of their tines and main beams. The truth is, bucks often rub the back of their tines and beams on brush and saplings as often as they do the front of them.

One of Charlie's photos captured this behavior perfectly. After getting Charlie's permission, my father made a drawing from the photo, left, for my chapter endings.

To illustrate how much some bucks rub the back of their antlers, I thought I'd share the photo at right from Ontario biologist Bruce Ranta. Bruce killed this old buck near his home in Kenora. It's fascinating to see how this old buck wore down the back of its antlers all the way to the cortex. This spot shows the junction of a brow tine with the main beam.

Bruce Ranta

EFFECTIVE TACTICS
FOR HUNTING BIG BUCKS

Aggressive Whitetail Hunting
by Greg Miller
Answers any hunter's questions on how to hunt trophy bucks in public forests and farmlands, as well as in exclusive hunting lands. It's the perfect approach for gun and bow hunters who don't have the time or finances to hunt exotic locales.
Softcover • 6 x 9 • 208 pages
80 b&w photos
AWH01 • $14.95

Proven Whitetail Tactics
by Greg Miller
Both entertaining and educational, this volume, from one of America's premier deer hunters, explains effective strategies for scouting, calling and stalking white-tailed deer in the close-to-home locales available to most hunters. Packed with tips and tactics that spell deer hunting success.
Softcover • 6 x 9 • 224 pages
100 b&w photos
AWH02 • $19.95

The Deer Hunters
Tactics, Lore, Legacy and Allure of American Deer Hunting
by Patrick Durkin, Editor
Liberally illustrated in dynamic full-color, this coffee-table treasure examines effective deer hunting strategies and the mystique surrounding the magnificent whitetail. Also provides a thought-provoking look at hunting ethics in the 1990s, and the common bonds shared by hunters, the whitetail and the land.
Hardcover • 8-1/2 x 11 • 208 pages
110 color photos
BOD • $29.95

SATISFACTION GUARANTEE
If for any reason you are not completely tisfied with your purchase, simply return it within 14 days and receive a full refund, less shipping.

Shipping and Handling:
$3.25 1st book; $2 ea. add'l. Call for UPS delivery rates.
Foreign orders $15 per shipment plus $5.95 per book.
Sales tax: CA 7.25%, VA 4.50%, IA 6.00%, PA 6.00%, TN 8.25%, WA 8.20%, WI 5.50%, IL 6.25%

Credit Card Customers Call Toll-free
800-258-0929 Dept. OTB9
M-F, 7 am - 8 pm • Sat, 8 am - 2 pm, CST
Krause Publications, 700 E. State Street • Iola, WI 54990-0001
www.krause.com
ealers call M-F 8 am - 5 pm CT, 888-457-2873 ext. 880 for information and a FREE all-product catalog!

DISCOVER SECRETS TO WHITETAIL BEHAVIOR

Whitetail Behavior Through the Seasons
by Charles J. Alsheimer
More than 160 striking action shots reveal a rarely seen side of North America's most impressive game animal. In-the-field observations will help you better understand all aspects of the whitetail deer, from breeding to bedding. Nature lovers and hunters will love this stunning book.
Hardcover • 9 x 11-1/2 • 208 pages
166 color photos
WHIT • $34.95

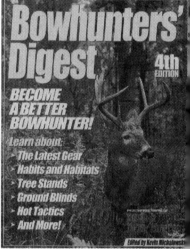

Bowhunters' Digest
4th Edition
Edited by Kevin Michalowski
Hit the woods armed with the latest tactical information designed to make you a better bowhunter. This fully updated edition will help you find active deer, choose a perfect stand location and put your broadhead right where it counts. You know nothing tops the thrill of setting your sight pin behind the shoulder of a monster buck. Now, some of America's hottest hunters share their tips to help you achieve the bowhunting success you've always dreamed of.
Softcover • 8-1/2 x 11
288 pages
300 b&w photos
BOW4 • $19.95

Whitetails by the Moon
by Charles J. Alsheimer, edited by Patrick Durkin
Charles J. Alsheimer, Deer & Deer Hunting magazine's Northern field editor, explains how deer hunters can use autumn moon cycles to predict peak times in the North and South to hunt rutting white-tailed bucks. He details the ground-breaking research conducted that unlocke the mysteries of the moon's influence on deer activity and behavior.
Softcover • 6 x 9 • 208 pages
100 b&w photos
LUNAR • $19.95

SATISFACTION GUARANTEE	Shipping and Handling:
If for any reason you are not completely satisfied with your purchase, simply return it within 14 days and receive a full refund, less shipping.	$3.25 1st book; $2 ea. add'l. Call for UPS delivery rates. Foreign orders $15 per shipment plus $5.95 per book. **Sales tax:** CA 7.25%, VA 4.50%, IA 6.00%, PA 6.00%, TN 8.25%, WA 8.20%, WI 5.50%, IL 6.25%

Credit Card Customers Call Toll-free
800-258-0929 Dept. OTB9
M-F, 7 am - 8 pm • Sat, 8 am - 2 pm, CST
Krause Publications, 700 E. State Street • Iola, WI 54990-0001
www.krause.com
Dealers call M-F 8 am - 5 pm CT, 888-457-2873 ext. 880 for information and a FREE all-product catalog

Get THREE magazines in one with

DEER & DEER HUNTING
MAGAZINE

DEER & DEER HUNTING
magazine contains practical
and comprehensive information for ALL white-tailed deer
hunters.
DEER & DEER HUNTING
is everything you want or need
to know about the sport of
white-tailed deer hunting.
You won't need to buy separate
magazines about deer, bow
and gun hunting.
DEER & DEER HUNTING
covers it all. Subscribe today.
**It's like getting three
magazines in one!**

Gun Hunting   *Bow Hunting*   *Whitetail Hunting*

1 year *(9 issues)*
only
$19.95

Plus
receive a *Deer & Deer Hunting* almanac
FREE with your paid subscription,
a $6.95 value

**DEER &
DEER HUNTING**
MAGAZINE

ORDER TODAY!
Subscription Hotline
800-258-0929 *Dept. ABAWD6*

M - F 7 a.m. - 8 p.m. Sat. 8 a.m. - 2 p.m. CST
Krause Publications
700 E. State St., Iola, WI 54990-0001   *Write for foreign rates.*

Visit our web site: www.deeranddeerhunting.com

If you enjoyed *Greg Miller's Rub-Line Secrets*, you'll want to absorb even more of his insights into hunting America's No. 1 big-game animal, the white-tailed deer. Here's what hunters are saying about Greg's earlier books, *Aggressive Whitetail Hunting* and *Proven Whitetail Tactics*:

"I love reading about your strategies and hunting methods. There's no doubt that the advice I've gotten from your books will contribute to my future successes."
— Jody Hadachek,
Manhatten, Kansas

"Thank you very much for *Proven Whitetail Tactics*. I found myself moving from chapter to chapter, page to page, sentence to sentence and word to word — as if I were in the act of scouting itself."
— Mike Marek,
Ann Arbor, Mich.

"Your book *Proven Whitetail Tactics* has put me back on track. Your way of explaining deer hunting ideas is very straight-forward and easy to understand."
— Dino Nardi,
Sault Ste. Marie, Canada

"I really have enjoyed reading your books, and I appreciate a lot of your philosophies and your approach to deer hunting. I hold many of the same ideas."
— Mark Goodpaster,
Indianapolis, Ind.

"I'm a bit more experienced and well-read than the average bow-bender, and I found your book to be the best I've ever read. I've never written to an author before, but I feel that a 'thank you' note is appropriate."
— Rick Semrad,
Grafton, Wis.

"Once I started reading your book I found it hard to put it aside and go to bed. I know the information you've provided will be extremely beneficial to me in the seasons ahead. Thanks again!"
— Brian Hannon,
Lewistown, Pa.

"I was under the impression that I already was a good deer hunter. But reading your book made me more aware and alert to what I really need to be looking for in the woods. As a result, I've taken two trophy bucks in the past two years."
— Dean Jorgensen,
Ridgeway, Wis.

"I wanted to drop you a line to let you know how much I enjoyed your book. I've read a bunch of deer hunting books over the years, but I liked yours the best. It was full of good information and easy to understand."
— David Gilbertson,
Neenah, Wis.

Call Krause Publications today and order your copies of *Aggressive Whitetail Hunting* and *Proven Whitetail Tactics*.